BUILDING THE
VALUE MACHINE

BUILDING THE
VALUE MACHINE

Transforming your business through
collaborative customer partnerships

Peter Cheverton

**KOGAN
PAGE**

London and Philadelphia

First published in Great Britain and the United States in 2010 by Kogan Page Limited

Kogan Page Limited
120 Pentonville Road
London N1 9JN
United Kingdom
www.koganpage.com

Kogan Page US
525 South 4th Street, #241
Philadelphia PA 19147
USA

© Peter Cheverton, 2010

The right of Peter Cheverton to be identified as the author of this work has been asserted by him in accordance with the Copyright, Designs and Patents Act 1988.

ISBN   978 0 7494 5485 2

British Library Cataloguing-in-Publication Data

A CIP record for this book is available from the British Library.

Library of Congress Cataloging-in-Publication Data

Cheverton, Peter.
  Building the value machine : transforming your business through collaborative customer partnerships / Peter Cheverton. -- 1st ed.
    p. cm.
  Includes index.
  ISBN 978-0-7494-5485-2
  1. Leadership. 2. Marketing. 3. Customer services. I. Title.
  HD57.7.C488 2009
  658.4--dc22
                                            2009020556

Typeset by Saxon Graphics Ltd, Derby
Printed and bound in India by Replika Press Pvt Ltd

Cust/Add: 240950003/02   TGHR-T   UNIVERSITY OF GUELPH
Cust PO No.   91420   Cust Ord Date: **14-Dec-2009**
BBS Order No: **C1197781**   Ln: **29**   Del: **1**   BBS Ord Date: **14-Dec-2009**
0749454857-41821238   Sales Qty: **1**   #Vols: **001**
(9780749454852)

Building the value machine

Subtitle: **transforming your business through collabor**   Stmt of Resp: **Peter Cheverton.**

HARDBACK   Pub Year: **2010**   Vol No.:   _____   Edition:

Cheverton, Peter   Ser. Title:

Kogan Page
Acc Mat:

Profiled	**Barcode Label Applicati**	**Affix Security Device US**	**Spine Label Protector U!**
Tech	**Base Charge Processing**	**Security Device US**	**TechPro Cataloging US**
Services:	**Circulation (Author/Titl**	**Affix Spine Label US**	
	Property Stamp US	**Spine Label BBS US**	

Fund: **BLKW-1604**   Location: **BLKW-1604**

Stock Category: Department: **BLKW-1604**

Class #:   Cutter: Collection:

Order Line Notes:

Notes to Vendor:

Blackwell Book Services

Contents

About the author

Peter Cheverton is a founding Director of INSIGHT Marketing and People, a global training and consultancy firm specializing in the development of customer-focused business strategies, with a strong focus on Key Account Management, Global Account Management, and Business Leadership. He has developed an international reputation as one of the leading experts in these challenging areas, working 'hands on' with clients in Europe, the Americas, AsiaPacific and Africa.

Peter spends much of his time helping clients with the practical implementation of their business strategies, as well as presenting INSIGHT's *Key Account Management Masterclass* around the globe, including events in London, Paris, Brussels, Stockholm, Oslo, Vienna, Budapest, Prague, Warsaw, Shanghai, Beijing, Singapore, Kuala Lumpur, Seoul, Tokyo, Melbourne, Boston, New York and Chicago.

Prior to establishing INSIGHT in 1991, Peter was the European Sales and Marketing Manager for Dulux Paints.

For contact details please see the section on 'Getting Further Help' at the end of the book.

Foreword

This book builds on three of my earlier titles (all published by Kogan Page): *Key Marketing Skills*, from which comes the process of matching the supplier's capabilities to the needs of the customer, *Key Account Management*, from which comes the principle of regarding Key and Key Development Accounts as vitally important investments, and *Understanding Brands*, from which comes the idea of the brand as a relationship made up of a series of interactions with customers.

It is always pleasing to be told by a client that they have used your books to improve their business, but it seems that the same obstacles always arise at the point of implementation, two particular 'sins' of modern business: short-termism resulting from an overly narrow conception of the selling task, and poor leadership. My motivation in writing this new book has been the desire to act on those two sins.

It is not that the senior managers have in themselves been poor (I should quickly say, for any that might be reading this, that I have met many that are truly excellent), rather that the circumstances they find themselves in have prevented them from taking their proper place in things. So much time is given to budget control, performance monitors and all the tools of managing 'today', that little time is left for managing 'tomorrow', or to use the proper description of that task: little time is left for *leading*.

This book is firmly rooted in the need for leadership teams to make better use of some of their key investments – almost certainly the most important investments that any business has – their most important customers.

Acknowledgements

My thanks go to the many excellent clients of INSIGHT Marketing and People Ltd with whom I have worked since 1991. Their efforts in building their own value machines have provided the inspiration for this book.

Part I

The Value Machine

1

The value machine

Value is in the eye of the beholder – we know it to be true. Take two apparently equal 'great ideas' and a customer will very likely see one as valuable, and the other as not. It's got little to do with the quality of the ideas as they leave the supplier; it's got everything to do with how they arrive at the customer – how they impact on that customer's circumstances.

So, value happens *within* the customer – we also know that to be true – which is why the customer is king, the focal point of our attention, and the most important piece in the whole business jigsaw.

But is it really so?

Most people seem to think so. It's a notion that has been beaten into us for so long that any other possibility has to seem absurd, almost heretical. Attend any cross-functional management meeting and sooner or later someone (usually from Sales) is going to say something like: 'It's the customers that matter, you know, the people out there, the people who pay our salaries'. Sound about right?

Sure, but where does this get you? For a start your competitors are looking to just the same customers, and what do you think your competitors are saying to themselves about this issue of who pays *their* salaries?

It is said that competitive advantage comes from the true understanding of the customer's needs. After many years of saying just such things myself, at every opportunity provided, I am not about to disagree, but the statement does not go far enough; it doesn't complete the task. A customer might be very helpful, in their own interest, in giving a supplier absolutely clear instructions on what they regard as valuable – but what if that instruction is given with equal clarity to all competing suppliers; where then is the competitive advantage in that?

Value *starts* with knowledge of the customer, but that is only the beginning of the pursuit of a unique value proposition, and so true competitive advantage. If anything is to come of this vital spark of knowledge, what we might call a *customer insight*, then it has to kindle a flame within the supplier's organization, a flame that sets light to the supplier's internal resources. True competitive advantage has to come from within the supplier's organization; if you are a supplier then it has to be about *you*.

Does this sound dangerous ground? For years we have been urged by all and sundry to focus on the world outside, not inside, which has been good advice for those businesses that found the fluff in their own navels more fascinating than what went on behind the closed doors of their customers.

But having now learned to look outside, to see and understand the customer's needs, we find that this is not enough. We know that value happens *inside* the customer, but it has to be *created* somewhere else – inside the supplier's organization – and this is where things often go awry.

Ask any sales professional how they feel about the 'internal functions' of their business and prepare yourself for a stream of invective. This is where all *their* great ideas get stuck, mangled or ignored, and don't forget, these were the ideas that came from the customer-focused end of the business: the sales team. That's what they say.

Ask those internal functions how they feel about the sales professionals in their business and be prepared for more invective. These are the people who don't seem to understand what is possible, or even more importantly, what is good for our business. Why don't they chase the right kind of opportunities – the ones that suit us? That's what they say.

Let's not argue about who is right or wrong (there is often enough guilt on both sides to have the whole business condemned), but focus on what has to be done about it.

THE 'RIGHT KIND' OF VALUE

This book will argue that the really important issues really do exist *inside* the supplier's own organization. Their challenge is to find the 'right kind' of leadership that will foster the 'right kind' of collaborative working and planning processes that will allow the creation of the 'right kind' of value, and yes, with the 'right kind' of customers.

Any fool can 'delight their customers' – just cut your prices in half and send out a customer satisfaction survey to see how easy it can be – but that's not the challenge behind finding the right kind of value. The right kind of value is the kind that is good for the customer's business, and the kind that will be good for our own.

The business that thinks this way and pursues these goals is the sort of business that will be described in this book – the business that wishes to become a true _value machine_.

HOW GOOD MUST WE BE?

We will address, and help answer I hope, a number of important questions:

- How good will we need to be at observing and predicting the customer's true needs?
- How good will we need to be at selecting from those _opportunities_ the ones that match our current capabilities, and even more importantly, the ones that will help us build new capabilities?
- How good will we need to be at taking those twin insights – customer focused and internally focused – and using them to develop new business strategies?
- How good will we need to be at communicating those strategies across the breadth of our own business, ensuring that everyone involved can develop their own functional plans to create the value propositions required?
- How good will we need to be at developing those value propositions _alongside_ the customer, through the 'scary' process (scary for some) of customer collaboration?
- And how good will we need to be at delivering on our promises to the customer – those famous _moments of truth_ – and ensuring the appropriate rewards to our own organization?

In answering these questions, and by noting the gap between ideal and current performance, you will come to your own priorities as to what needs to be done. It isn't necessary to be good at everything, but it is vital to be good at those things that matter. Determining the difference is one of the first tasks for the leadership team.

FROM GOOD TO GREAT...

Good ideas are to be found all around us – your own business will be sitting on plenty (though sometimes they lurk in unexpected corners) – but by addressing the questions posed above we give ourselves the chance of developing them into truly great ideas.

We all like to celebrate those truly great ideas, the ones that change the whole nature of value in business – the development of mass production (and prices to match needs), the invention of the globally merchandized consumer brand (and needs to match prices), the creation of the World Wide Web – and looking for the personal inspiration that lay behind them has always been a source of fascination for ambitious business folk. But in seeking to replicate them such ambition is often thwarted, and not due to any lack of personal brilliance but because the source of their true greatness is misunderstood. The real celebrations should not be about individual entrepreneurs but about the great businesses and the great processes within those businesses that turned good ideas into great ones.

Sadly, most processes are duller than most people (note I say 'most') but we ignore them at our peril. Putting our faith in personal inspiration is too easy; we have to face the hard graft of making things happen through the sometimes-grinding gears of the business organization. Processes are necessary, and when they can be made to be great processes then things start to run a little smoother. Business processes are rather like the well-oiled technique of a truly great comedian, the sweat and tears that lie behind those oh-so-simple punchlines. They say that comedy is 5 per cent inspiration and 95 per cent perspiration. Well, that goes for business too...

This book aims to chart the path of perspiration, but there is also some good news for those who favour the inspiration route. Once the right leadership is in place, and once the whole business is aligned behind the same strategy, it's funny how inspiration starts to occur more readily, that is to say, the 'right kind' of inspiration.

JETTISONING THE BAGGAGE

All of this comes at a price, and part of that price will be the jettisoning of some rather old and timeworn baggage. Never easy, and particularly so when the 'baggage' in question worked quite serviceably, in its day. Baggage is to do with people – somebody always owns it – and a great deal of pride and ego will be found wrapped around it.

Always remember: those people who grew up with 'what once worked', and benefited from it by being good at it – well, those are the people now in charge. So who's going to talk to them about being rid of 'old baggage'? It takes real guts to tackle the bosses in this way, but perhaps even more courage is required from the bosses themselves; getting rid of baggage is often about getting rid of their own past. The true value machine depends on such leadership 'guts'.

In particular it's time to leave behind one of the most venerable of business tools – the famous four P's of marketing. For too long otherwise clever companies have tried to shoehorn their activities into these four 'boxes', as if they were some untouchable and inviolate quartet. But now it's time to break out; the days of doing things 'to' our customers – through our *products*, our *price*, and our *promotion*, while keeping those customers firmly in their *place* – are fading fast; now we must aim to collaborate 'with' our customers, in pursuit of truly customer-focused value propositions.

Of course, it remains easier to do things the old way, the way of the four P's. Doing things '*to*' customers, and better still without their knowledge until it happens to them, will always have an attraction for a supplier; the attraction of being in control. Everything feels a lot more comfortable, there are no conflicting agendas, no competing egos; it's just a pity that it doesn't work so well any more. (We will consider some alternatives to the four P's in Chapter 8.)

But doing things '*with*' the customer is not as easy as it sounds. Customers can steal good ideas and pass them on to cheaper competitors. Customers can be short term. Customers can lie. Such are the realities of life, realities that make true customer partnerships a rarity – but then we are not proposing that this is something that must be done with every customer – customers are not equal – some customers are a good deal more equal than others… and those of course are the right kind of customers.

THE VALUE MACHINE MODEL

The challenge of building a business that can set loose the power and creativity of its internal functions to work with customers in pursuit of better value propositions is captured in the model shown in Figure 1.1 – what we will call the *Value Machine Model*.

The model describes a business that knows how to *target* its customers, recognizing that as *investments* some customers promise a better return than others. 'Returns' can mean many things – volume, revenue, margin, share of business, access to new opportunities (to name but a few) – but are not limited to the customer in question. Some customers are even more important and valuable, being of benefit not just in themselves but to the whole business, even to other customers… We might call these our true *Key Accounts*, about which a good deal more will be said in Chapters 5 and 6.

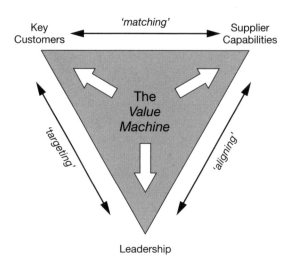

Figure 1.1   *The value machine model*

The model describes a business that knows how to *match* its own capabilities to the needs of the customer, learning how to enhance those capabilities as required, in pursuit of a unique match between supplier and customer. It does so with a steady eye on the changing nature of the customer's business and market, and an equally steady eye on the 'money-making-logic' of its own business. The skills required to effect these ideal matches will be described in Chapters 7, 8 and 9.

The model describes a business that knows how to *align* all the relevant functions behind that targeting, and behind the pursuit of those unique matches. It achieves this through a leadership that is alive to the dynamics of the market, the customer, and their own business.

The result is a business that has done away with the invective of the sales team blaming the internal functions, or the internal functions berating the sales team.

It is a business where the customer is something more than 'king'. Instead of pretending that the customer is always right (a pretence that we never fully accept, and so rebel against – so negating the whole notion), we can now regard the customer (right and wrong) as the source of our business wisdom; they are our means of ensuring that we are doing the right things.

It is a business that knows how to learn, developing its processes and its value propositions through both the rigours of hard experience and the joys of accidental discovery.

It is a business that knows how to convert the great mass of market and customer data (a mass that sometimes threatens to sink a business in a bog of procrastination) into clear insights from which to form the foundations of its business strategy.

It is a business that can take that strategy all the way down to the nitty-gritty actions of making it happen.

It is a business that some would call 'lucky', but not because of any unusual good fortune, rather, because it has learned to make its own luck.

It is a business that demands great leadership. As well as providing a crystal clear strategic vision it must also focus on getting things done – two very different mindsets that the philosophy of the value machine helps bring closer together, and without falling into the trap of 'command and control'. The measure of their true 'greatness' will in fact be found in their ability to 'let go'.

It is a business that requires a new language to express its motivations and mechanics, and it is to the leadership team that most will look to provide the new vocabulary. Much then is demanded of that leadership team: an understanding of the vital linkages between the world outside and the delivery capabilities inside – an ability to break down the barriers between functions – an ability to coach their teams towards new ways of collaborative working, both internally and externally. And here we find the need for that new language. In a true value machine those two words, 'internal' and 'external', might seem as old fashioned and anachronistic as those famous four P's…

2

Leadership – the pivotal activity

The public face of most businesses is as well presented as a catwalk model. PR firms are paid well enough to ensure the triple gloss of modernity, corporate unity and energetic resolve, all the way from the Armani-suited board to the Primark-clad tele-sales office. Yet we all know the truth that lies beneath the surface: the creaking systems and processes (inherited from some chap called Noah), the interdepartmental rivalries and competing management egos, and the huge energies expended in the search for functional dominance by one player over another. If this sounds rather too much like the synopsis from a TV business soap opera, then take a close look at your own business; is it collaboration or competition that makes things tick?

It can be argued that tensions and rivalries between functions are the source of much creativity, healthy competition indeed, but too often it is a case of putting a retrospective gloss on what was simply a sorry squabble. I am reminded of one such 'squabble' that lasted over a year, a squabble that had 'good intentions' on both sides, but the sort of good intentions that served only to place obstacles in the way of a satisfactory resolution to a genuine customer issue.

A speciality chemicals business had delivered high-value stock to its customers at 48-hours' notice for many years, and had a good, but not spotless, record for delivering on time and in full – the famous OTIF. For some while the sales team had been receiving signals from the customer that a move to 24-hours' notice was required, the customer wishing to reduce the burden of a particularly high-cost inventory. The sales team were keen to help but had been slow to respond, guessing at the likely negative response from their colleagues at HQ. At monthly sales meetings there had developed a ritual castigation of the folk in distribution: 'yet another obstacle in our path...'

Unbeknown to the sales team the distribution folk had in fact been considering a change to delivery response times, and in pursuit of the same goal – customer satisfaction. They recognized the importance of OTIF performance, they were after all the people who received the reports, and the complaints (and of late, the threatened penalty charges) of OTIF failings. They set their eyes on a 100 per cent OTIF record, and were certain they could achieve it if they moved the guaranteed delivery response time to 72 hours.

And so began the 'squabble'. Both sides had good intentions – the satisfaction of the customer – and both sides claimed a knowledge of the customer's true desires. The sales team claimed their 'knowledge' based on what they were told, while the distribution team claimed their 'knowledge' based on the professional logic of 'any right-thinking logistics manager'.

Who was right? Were the distribution folk doing a fine impersonation of an ostrich with their 'head-in-the-sands' attitude, based on their own performance criteria? Were the sales folk simply parroting their customer's demands with an uncritical ear?

The final answer was a compromise. The supplier settled on a promise of 100 per cent OTIF deliveries at 72-hours' notice, with the agreement to manage consignment stock at the customers' premises. So, was this a creative outcome resulting from the tensions between the two functions, or a suboptimal outcome resulting from their mutual intransigence? It was certainly an expensive outcome, as anyone who has calculated the cost of consignment stock (and particularly those that involve high-value items) will testify. More to the point, it wasn't what the customer wanted. They wanted deliveries at 24-hours' notice, just as they had told the sales people. This was required not only to reduce their working capital, but also to free up warehouse space that could be given to lower value items where large orders meant big discounts. Some of those orders might even come the way of their reluctant supplier... if only... but unfortunately the sales people, in their eagerness to win the internal battle, never enquired down that alley...

We find in this case study a common sin – the development of a business strategy (the provision of consignment stock) without any true insight into the nature of the customer's ambitions, or, for that matter, the supplier's own best interests. We will return to this sin in Chapter 3 when considering the nature of strategic planning, but for now let us just consider it an example of the downsides of a business that, through a process of argument and fudge, fails on three points:

1. failure to understand the customer's true ambitions (listening is not enough);
2. failure to align their functions behind customer-focused goals;
3. failure to seek outcomes that serve their own best interests.

We might add a fourth: a failure of leadership.

So far we have been considering the perils of squabbles between functions, but what of that equally perilous situation: the overly dominant function? Whether due to history or the strength of particular personalities, it is quite common for one function to gain the 'upper hand' in a business, often reflected in, and maintained by, the career histories of the members of the management team. In the short term such dominance can work to the benefit of the business, perhaps reflecting specific market circumstances.

The 1970s and 1980s saw the emergence and rapid growth of a new kind of retailer in the UK DIY market – the out-of-town superstore. Their business model was radically different from the existing customer base (largely smaller scale specialist outlets) and demanded a very different supplier response both in terms of products and services.

No surprise that in such a circumstance the suppliers' sales functions should play an increasingly dominant role, taking on the mantle of Key Account Management, aiming to understand the new business model and translate its requirements to their colleagues in marketing, R&D, manufacturing and logistics. All went well for many years as retailer growth fuelled a sales bonanza.

And then the new customers reached saturation point; with an out-of-town superstore on practically every ring road roundabout, a new era had begun – consolidation, acquisition and merger created even more powerful, and yet more fiercely competitive customers. The lack of real revenue growth created all sorts of new demands on suppliers; demands that to the suppliers (that is, the sales people in the suppliers) seemed entirely unreasonable.

The retailers wanted new products to be designed exclusively for them, they wanted supplier display materials to their own corporate design, they wanted daily deliveries and changes to the ordering process that gave them direct access to the suppliers' operational processes. The sales folk saw these demands as an assault on their brands, on their profitability, and not least on their position of power within their own organization. Rather than airing these demands with their colleagues (the only people who could make them happen) they closed down the lines of communication and trained their sales professionals in 'tough negotiation' techniques.

And so the relationship became more volatile, the demands grew in their scope and intensity, and the suppliers (that is, the sales people in the suppliers) dug in their heels yet deeper.

The retailers were encouraged to forge ahead with their plans for own-brand development (including a high level of product innovation), to take charge of their own store layouts and presentational styles, and to design revolutionary solutions to their logistical challenges, and all pretty much without the help of their reluctant suppliers.

As the retailers' own-brands developed apace so the sales people in the premium branded suppliers began to speak of their customers as their biggest competitors, a language that could only serve to turn heads ever more inwardly. The language used was indeed telling – these were not proper brands, they were 'own-labels or private labels or plain no-labels', and clearly inferior and to be despised. Hardly a good starting point for customer relationships, and perhaps a whole decade of potential collaboration was lost.

This case study shows how in the longer term a mono-functional dominance can lead to problems. The dominant sales teams became a barrier rather than a conduit, and the other functions in the suppliers could only look on in sterile frustration. One of the great ironies of this period was the fact that many 'internal' functions were growing in their desire to be involved with the customer and had new ideas to bring to the table that would allow suppliers to participate in the customer's new agenda, but were prevented from so doing by their sales colleagues: 'We don't collaborate with the competition...'.

Where was the business leadership in all this? Where was the hand on the tiller that could see the approaching storm and call for a new setting of sails? The sorry truth was that in too many cases it was buried beneath the structural and cultural dominance of the sales function. In one case the Sales Director had even succeeded in establishing a completely separate office, many miles away from the 'interfering eyes' and 'meddlesome hands' of the rest of the business – an office referred to as 'the bunker'; a name entirely descriptive of the mentality that went with it.

If we return to the Value Machine Model introduced in Chapter 1, we can begin to see what is going on. Figure 2.1 shows the value machine in balance, matching the needs of the customers with the creation of appropriate value through the internal functions.

Figure 2.2 illustrates the business out of balance, weighed down by the dominance of inwardly looking functions and so 'leaning' in their direction to the eventual detriment of the customers' sense of satisfaction. Ironically, in the case discussed it was the sales team – the group normally most likely to be

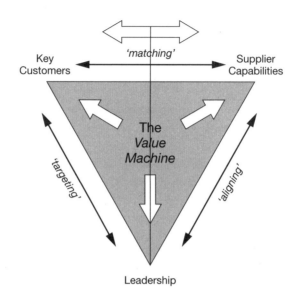

Figure 2.1   *The value machine in balance*

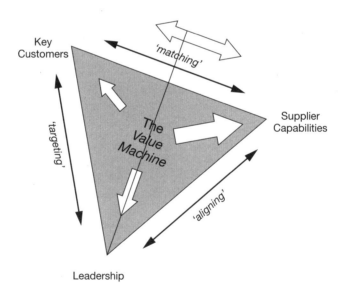

Figure 2.2   *The value machine out of balance*

outwardly facing – whose language and behaviours encouraged the inward-looking behaviours of the whole supplier business.

A business can just as easily lean in the other direction of course, with a bias towards the customer. A less damaging circumstance you might think, but not so. An 'out of balance' business is a business heading for problems, whichever way it leans, they're simply different problems…

Consider first the lean to the right, favouring the internal functions over and above the customers' needs. On the plus side, at least in the short term, we might see increasing efficiencies, better utilization of assets, reduced costs of manufacture and supply, but what of the longer term? As customers start to sense a lack of attention to their needs, perhaps an aloofness in the supplier, maybe even an arrogance (often accompanied by public 'boasts' of how efficient they are – never let the CEO be interviewed by the business press on such topics!), so they start to take their business elsewhere. Soon the short-term gains start to pale into insignificance against the problems of falling revenues, declining market share, and then of course the rising costs and internal inefficiencies…

So what of the lean to the left? Here a business focuses its attentions on the customer (who of course is _not_ always right), and to excess. 'Anything goes', and the resultant increase in demands placed on the supplier – whether for new products, variations on themes, or enhanced services – starts to take its toll on the internal functions. Mistakes start to occur, deadlines get missed, and step by step the customer begins to feel less satisfied, and all due to your desire to satisfy them beyond their wildest dreams…

Managers who have spent their formative years in such a situation, and have seen the consequences, often tend towards a rather belligerent stance with regard to customers. I have heard one say: 'Don't tell me that they pay our salaries, its only because we've resisted their damaging demands that we have salaries in the first place.' It's a view, and a view of experience.

Of course, take a manager who has grown up suffering the consequences of the opposite imbalance – the lean to the right – and we might witness one of those zealots for customer intimacy: 'and damn the consequences for those navel gazers at head office…'. Another view, and again, a view of experience.

Perhaps the single most important point to draw from these illustrations is the pivotal role (quite literally) of leadership. It is the responsibility of the leadership team to rise above the competing egos of their functional heads, and to rise above the potential prejudices of their own historical experiences – there is no room for favouritism in the value machine.

The leadership team has two clear responsibilities within the Value Machine Model:

- to focus the business on the right customers, and with the right degree of intensity;

- to align the internal functions behind that focus, and have them working in appropriate collaboration in order to create the appropriate value propositions.

It is a finely tuned task – the point at the bottom of the value machine triangle is indeed a fulcrum on which a business could wobble quite distressingly. Some businesses wobble and vacillate so much that their staff (not to mention their customers) suffer from a kind of motion sickness.

It is a task made harder by the fact that times change. What is the right balance for today may not be right for tomorrow, and given that the leadership team should be far more concerned with tomorrow (they have managers to manage today) they will almost inevitably be inducing some form of sea-sickness from time to time. Never an easy task, sniped at from all sides, particularly when the occasional *deliberate* imbalance is required, in order to deal with changes in the business environment. But hang on, didn't I say that an 'out of balance' business is a business heading for problems? Well I did, but what I should have said was: *unless it is deliberate*.

A service provider (an 'Institute' no less) offering formal qualifications in a number of professional and management areas suffered a poor reputation for its lack of flexibility. This inflexibility was, so they argued, actually a benefit. This takes some explaining.

In order for the qualifications to mean anything they had to be universal, standardized, and measured by immovable criteria. There was no room for tailoring to customer requirements in such a situation, so they said. This attitude only served to increase their unpopularity; inflexibility through inability is one thing, but inflexibility through intent (and backed by claims of it being good for you) is quite another…

This was a business leaning so far to the right, favouring its own internal issues, and so weighed down by the inertia of those issues, that it was almost beyond change, but change was so clearly required. The management team appreciated that they couldn't just flip the business back up into a balanced state, and indeed, any such effort would seriously compromise the ability of some of the internal functions to operate effectively.

The chosen solution was ingenious. Rather than attempting a slow process of change across all customers, they decided to go for a very radical change, but with only a very few customers. Having first identified a small number of Key Accounts (defined as customers who were not necessarily big, but were influential – let's call them 'change agents') they chose to focus their efforts with those customers in ways that could only be described as 'leaning to the left with a vengeance'.

Described variously as a pilot exercise, a piece of research, even a plain experiment, the real purpose was more politically adroit than that description suggested. By forcing changes in behaviours on a small and manageable front, it was possible to 'prove the case' for a new kind of customer focus, and so build momentum for more general change across all customer relationships.

It was an example of what I call *political entrepreneurship*: doing the possible in the face of the impossible while in pursuit of a well-identified opportunity. It required a deliberate imbalance to the Value Machine Model, but in a closely managed environment. Such a strategy would have been impossible without sanction from the top – this was an organization that would have eaten lone mavericks alive. It was a strategy that had to be actively led by the leadership team. The role of leadership in this regard was truly pivotal.

3

Fuelling the value machine

If we picture the value machine as just that, a machine, perhaps a great loco-motive, then the leadership team fulfil the role of the engineer, keeping it on the rails with judicious application of power and brakes (and of course, this being a very modern locomotive, it is of the tilting variety...).

They also come armed with a giant oilcan, the management and operational processes that keep the thing running smoothly, and the faster and more powerful the locomotive, the greater the need for top quality lubrication.

But what of the fuel: what powers the machine? This chapter will examine two significant ingredients (and there are others – see Chapter 7) that make up the chemistry of this hybrid fuel:

- Ingredient No. 1: the raw *data* of our business operations and activities – the things that we know about our own organization, its mechanics, its 'money-making logic', its strengths and its weaknesses.
- Ingredient No. 2: the raw *data* of our customer experiences – the things that we know about our markets, the players, their ambitions, their needs, their opportunities and the threats.

You will doubtless have recognized the elements of the classic SWOT analysis (strengths, weaknesses, opportunities, threats), a familiar tool that we will explore in a new form later in this chapter.

The chapter will also examine two vital processes (the oil in the machine) that are required if the fuel is to be put to work effectively:

1. A continuous cross-functional debate calling on new ways of thinking and new ways of behaving that will harness the creativity to be found in the collaboration, and necessary tensions, between those functions.
2. A business planning process that gives a context for this debate, and aims to turn the raw data of our operational and customer knowledge into clear and coherent strategies, by means of what we will call *strategic insights*.

Figure 3.1 shows how these ingredients and processes combine into a *business planning funnel*.

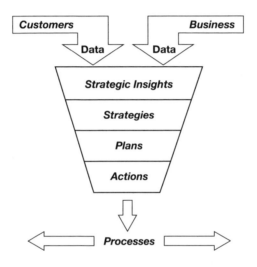

Figure 3.1   *The business planning funnel*

The planning funnel brings together the two fuel ingredients – *data* on our own operations and *data* on our customers – in pursuit of *strategic insights*. Too often these separate sources of information are kept apart from each other, the result of the silo-like structures of complex businesses. By combining them we aim to find where our internal capabilities can be harnessed to create true customer value, and what type of customer value can best contribute to our own wellbeing through profitable competitive advantage.

ENOUGH DATA...

The data is only the beginning of course, and we must resist the temptation to dwell too long on what is perhaps the easiest part of the process. Data is easy;

we know lots of stuff, particularly about ourselves, and if we take the time to put it together also about our customers. (I've often suspected that my clients already know pretty much everything they need to know about their customers, the only trouble is their 'knowledge' is held in hundreds of different heads – putting the jigsaw puzzle together is the problem to be solved.)

Thanks to various pieces of technology we can observe and record more such 'stuff' than ever before, and if we are not careful the very process of collecting and recording can become a fetish. I'm reminded of the advice with regard to market research: do enough such that you are able to make the decisions that need making, then stop; beyond that it is not necessary to go...

There comes a point when setting up yet another study, or finding yet another way to analyse and present the data, can become a hindrance rather than a help. When a business knows a great deal of stuff, analysis paralysis is always going to be a danger. Please don't think I am suggesting that ignorance is any kind of bliss; ignorance is always dangerous, but there is a balance to be found, and again we can see the role of the leadership team in determining just how much must be known before we know enough.

STRATEGIC INSIGHTS AND INTELLIGENT ANALYSIS

So, having determined that we have observed and recorded enough, the crucial question becomes: what to do with all that 'stuff'? At the risk of mixing my metaphors: how do we conjure up the alchemy of transformation – turning base metal 'data' into the gold of 'strategic insights'?

This only happens through *intelligent* analysis and debate. Note that I stress intelligent. This doesn't mean hiring a team of high-IQ consultants to do your thinking for you, but it does mean involving a team. At no other point in the process is there a greater need for breadth and variety of perspective. The debates and arguments of a cross-functional team, while sometimes seeming to hold us back, are in fact far more important at this stage than the single-minded certainties produced from a single function approach.

The prospect of intelligent analysis will be much improved if some form of disciplined process is observed (more oil to lubricate some grinding cross-functional gears). There are many such processes, each supported by its own analytical tool, each suiting different circumstances. I will highlight just one: the *shared future analysis*.

THE SHARED FUTURE ANALYSIS

The shared future analysis requires two sets of data, the very two sets that we have been discussing – data about our customers and data about ourselves. Figure 3.2 shows the matrix that we aim to complete and then subject to *intelligent analysis* in pursuit of those all-important strategic insights.

+ sign(s) we make a positive impact on their ambitions or reduce their worries	– sign(s) we detract from their ambitions, or compound their worries		The customer's opportunities and ambitions				The customer's threats and worries			
			1	2	3	4	1	2	3	4
Our strengths, as perceived by the customer	1			+++		+			+++	
	2									
	3		+++			++				
	4							++		+
Our weaknesses, as perceived by the customer	1						---		--	
	2									
	3		---			---				
	4							-		

Figure 3.2   *The shared future analysis*

First, we enter along the top of the matrix those things that we know to be our customers' ambitions, and those things that we know to be their worries. Remembering the SWOT analysis, these are the opportunities and the threats, but note that rather than the traditional use of this tool where the business considers its own opportunities and threats, we are using this tool to identify the opportunities and threats as seen by *our customers*.

I keep referring to 'our customers', but I don't of course mean all of our customers. We might use this analysis to consider those customers within a specific market segment where by definition they share similar needs and attitudes (see Chapter 4) or we might use it to consider just one customer, perhaps one of the Key Accounts that we will be discussing further in Chapters 5 and 6.

This is no easy task, putting ourselves in the shoes of the customer, and not least because it is at this point that we might find the weaknesses of our market segmentation process – they don't all share the same needs and attitudes! For this reason the single customer analysis might prove more effective. In identifying these ambitions and worries we have to do our best to rid our minds of thoughts of ourselves. We tend to colour our perceptions of the customer's needs by ideas of what we are able to do about them. It is very easy to ignore a customer ambition for which we can make no contribution. This tool is an attempt to escape from that easy trap, and to identify what thoughts occupy *their* minds: their true ambitions, and worries.

Now we can turn to the two boxes on the left-hand side – and here we can allow thoughts of our own business back into our heads, but only if we can picture it through our customers' eyes. We are trying here to identify what the customer thinks we are good at, and what we are poor at – our strengths and our weaknesses, as they perceive them.

Huge doses of honesty are required at this point, and a firm resolve not to be defensive. If they think you are poor at something that you are convinced you are good at, then for the purpose of this exercise you are poor. You may resolve to change their perceptions of course; that may be one of the positive outcomes from an insight provided by the analysis, but I am getting ahead of myself – for the moment it is about registering customer perceptions, not what it says in your supplier brochure.

Before turning to the next step in the analysis we might just ask: from where will all this data come? Inevitably it will be from a range of sources. Customer satisfaction surveys should throw plenty of light on our strengths and weaknesses, and should also (while they are about it, and if they are conducted properly) tell us much about the customers' ambitions and concerns. Don't limit your thinking by limiting your sources – of course the sales and customer service professionals should know about the customers' ambitions and worries but they are not the only people with a view. Knowledge of our weaknesses will come readily from people on the end of complaints, but what of our strengths? Who receives the telephone calls telling us how great we are? We need to range a bit further than that, and act a bit smarter: analyse the successes – who and what made them successes – was it the products, the services, or the way in which we presented them, or was it the way in which we developed them?

What we are discussing here is of course a cross-functional debate, and one that encourages people to look over the walls and fences of their traditional territories and functional interests.

Go ask the customer. Read company reports. Talk to the customer's customers. Ask your bosses, and ask your most junior staff – who do you think knows best, for instance, about the customer's perceptions regarding your deliveries: the head of distribution, or the truck drivers who get it in the neck when it goes wrong?

One last comment on the data stage; don't be shy about admitting what you don't know. This analysis is going to be used to form our business strategy and it would be as well if it isn't founded on guesses and assumptions. If you don't know, admit it, and then aim to find out.

Now let's return to the analysis, and the next step. Taking each strength in turn, we ask: how does it contribute to the customer's ambitions, and how does it reduce their worries? Doubtless some of the things identified as strengths have no impact on either of these issues – and what might that tell us about our view of that thing as a strength? Quite.

Where we _do_ make a positive impact, mark it with a cross, or three crosses if the impact is significant.

Do the same with the weaknesses, only using minuses this time to identify where we hold the customer back from an ambition, or worst of all, compound an existing worry. Once again, perhaps some weaknesses had no relevance to either ambitions or worries, and so the same question can be asked – what does that tell us about the significance of this weakness?

We now have a picture, a snapshot that tells us something about the likelihood, or not, of a shared future with the customer or customers under analysis. Are we a significant supplier making positive contributions (through our plusses), or do we hold the customer back, irritating them and disappointing them (through our minuses)?

If we have an analysis covered in minuses with barely a plus to be seen then this is time for some serious questions: can we remove those weaknesses, and will it be worth our while to do so?

Or perhaps we have an analysis covered in plusses and only a few minuses. Before celebrating, ask: are we properly rewarded for what we now see to be our true significance as a supplier, and, do those minuses detract from what should be a strong supplier position?

It is the ensuing debate that aims to take the _insights_ raised by the analysis and begin to translate them into a _business strategy_. As ever we will have options: where should we focus our efforts – removing negatives or accentuating the positives? Take those weaknesses – if removing them is largely a PR exercise to change customer perceptions then the decision and action might be relatively easy, whereas true fundamental weaknesses might require greater thought – do we tackle the weaknesses, or do we reassess the customer or segment? As for the strengths – what sort of reward should we seek for our brilliance?

In essence then, the shared future analysis is designed to help us manage our investments more effectively by helping weigh the options intelligently. Are we targeting the right customers, and with the right level of effort, and for an appropriate reward? Certainty those three things will bode well for the effective use of our fuel – our valuable data – and the next task will be to ensure that our value machine purrs with well-oiled efficiency.

OILING THE WHEELS

Of course something like this analysis goes on informally within individual functions pretty much all the time – it's called 'gossiping about the business'. Sales people are particularly advanced in the practice. Gossiping is fine, it's part of the lubrication of any value machine, but it should never be mistaken for the real thing – cross-functional debate. The problem with gossip is it tends to be carried out within the boundaries of a silo function, indeed it is one of the ways in which functions bond as teams, by developing their own unique way for talking about the business and its customers. The type of gossip, and the language used, defines the group, and as any anthropologist or social scientist would tell you, that makes all other groups look and sound a little foreign. This may explain some of the problems that occur when functions try to work together – they speak different languages.

The shared future analysis is an attempt to formalize the habit of gossip, and to turn it into a cross-functional habit. By establishing a common language it becomes so much easier for the resulting debates to be seen as the preliminary steps to the development of business strategy, and not random arguments about how we each see the world.

I don't want to pretend that cross-functional working is easy. There are many things that stand in its way and 'different languages' may turn out to be one of the lesser obstacles. High up on the list is *time*. It isn't so much lack of time (often a smokescreen to other issues) that is the problem, rather that different functions work to different timetables, and for very good reasons. What might be an empty diary period for one function – and so an *'obvious opportunity'* for some cross-functional work – might be the most frantic and frenetic time of the year for another. I once attended an early session of a newly forming cross-functional team where they ran through a whole year's diary without finding a week that was free for all present (and there were only six people in the room!).

Another apparent 'blocker' is the diversity of cultures within any one business. We often think of cultural diversity as something to be encountered only when working globally – the classic East versus West debate – but if you are looking for examples of cultural misunderstanding, perhaps even conflict, then look no further than the interactions between functions within any business. People are unique, infinitely variable, but put them in the 'tribes' of a sales team, or an R&D department, or a manufacturing hub, and let them develop their own language and behaviours, and you have culture writ large. The stereotypes may not turn out to be true – sales people may not be anecdote-spouting boosters, R&D folk may not be reclusive eggheads – but the preconceptions go before us all.

Truly effective cross-functional teams have learned to recognize the cultural differences and make of them what they truly are – benefits and advantages. This is why I called it only an 'apparent' blocker. Given time, patience, and understanding – three requirements all too often in short supply in the fury of modern business – cross-functional teams will grow to value the different approaches to issues and problems that different backgrounds and working experiences engender. The notorious 'away-day' really can help, if planned properly, and executed with care. The key is in the intentions expressed. These should not be excuses to expose fault or apportion blame, but opportunities to understand different viewpoints, and value them as a dynamic part of the business planning process.

Perhaps the real killer however is the fact that individual functions feel so much more confident of themselves when working alone. Left to themselves they will always do an excellent job, *by their own lights*. It is so much easier to take a view of the world from the perspective of an individual function – no complications, no contradictions – and having taken that focused view the *insights* and *strategy* follow easily and satisfyingly… but I think you can see where this is headed.

Consider just one business decision: the question of which customers should be regarded as our most important – the Key Accounts. Would we be surprised if manufacturing folk tended to favour customers that are large, and whose orders will fill the plant? The logistics folk might prefer customers who are regular and predictable, the sort you can build a distribution operation around. Might those from Marketing look to customers with dominant market positions? And Sales, they wouldn't be keen on those customers growing the fastest… would they? And so it goes on – the R&D department like customers with interesting challenges, and the customer services department favour customers that don't bother them with too many complaints…

This last point is of course a slur on the many excellent customer service departments who realize that the complaint, to use the well-worn cliché, can be a gift. And there is good news here. Most functions do better than their stereotypes, a lot better, through genuinely good intentions, and a real desire to contribute. If only such energy and goodwill can be harnessed, through strong leadership, then the value machine will be up and humming. In the absence of that leadership (and it is a sad observation to make) independent good intentions set alongside high levels of activity, and if separated from a shared strategy, can lead a business astray. Sometimes such isolated good intentions can be as damaging as bad intentions, which at least come with the advantage that nothing much happens as a result of them…

I recall having to go to the head of Distribution, many years ago, as a timid sales representative seeking a favour on behalf of my customer. Actually it was quite a significant favour, and I was none too confident of my case. The customer, a large retailer, was insisting that we should affix *their* price labels to our products before we made our deliveries to their stores up and down the country. This was clearly a request made long before the days of barcode scanners at checkouts, and was of significant value to the retailer as it would allow them to reduce staffing levels once all suppliers provided the same service. We were in fact one of the last suppliers not to have agreed, or, 'to be broken' was how I think they put it!

To my great surprise the normally ferocious head of Distribution (I think he was an ex Sergeant Major from the Royal Army Corp of Transport) was only too pleased to oblige. So pleased in fact, and with no hint of a struggle, that I went away completely oblivious of the additional costs I had just incurred, and as a result did nothing about getting any quid pro quo from the customer. My fault of course – I can only blame that head of Distribution for not putting me off!

But shouldn't he have been asking me what I was getting in return? Perhaps, but that was not how his mind was working. He had agreed so readily because he had read the runes of automation coming his way and was looking for something to occupy his people – a kind of insurance policy against redundancies and the shrinking of his empire. It also enlivened an otherwise dull job.

As a result we managed to deliver significant value to the customer and didn't look for so much as a thank you. I'm pretty sure, in retrospect, that the retailer must have thought us mad.

Of course, we were all looking at the thing from the wrong angle, the narrow angle of our own function. I was the nervous sales representative thinking I was after a favour for a customer. The head of Distribution was looking to do the best for his department.

Neither of us bothered to understand the other's issues, and so no strategic insights were drawn from our 'data': my knowledge of the value to the customer, his knowledge of the cost to our own organization, which by implication might have given us a quantifiable estimate of the value to the customer.

Oddly enough, it was the lack of friction between us that led to a poor outcome – there was no debate. There is a saying in Dutch that translates (very roughly and with the removal of some expletives) as: 'If there is no friction, then things just slide'. This was an example of a business 'sliding' into action, effortlessly implementing a new 'added value service', but with no proper understanding of that value and so no hope of winning the appropriate reward. I even think (and I shudder at the memory) that at our next sales meeting, when asked what I had gained, that I said something like: 'well, we kept the business', a truly pathetic phrase that should send alarm bells ringing in every head that hears it said.

If only sales reps would stop and think, once in a while, like distribution people, and if only distribution people would occasionally think like sales reps – wouldn't that get things done a little bit more effectively? I wish I'd said it at the time, but at least I can say it now, and the same goes for any other functions brought together to find valuable solutions for customers.

KNOWING YOUR TRUE VALUE

It is when we bring our own functions together that we begin to realize not only how clever we are but also how valuable we are. I recall once taking part in a cross-functional exercise where each functional team were asked to write down everything they did on sticky notes – one action per note – and then place them in chronological order on a blank wall. We then looked at each other's 'chains', and with a little rearranging managed to lay the whole thing out from start to finish. The overwhelming emotion in the room was something like: 'gosh, how complicated, isn't it amazing how anything ever gets done to completion – aren't we clever!'

The workings of any value machine will certainly be clever, but they should not be a surprise to anyone, not even a pleasant one. Use the journey towards its achievement to learn the truth about what each function can and does contribute to the dynamics of your own business. Use it to learn the needs of the customer, and then bring your two understandings together in a matching process that brings benefit and reward to both sides.

In case all this talk of data, shared futures, and planning funnels might seem a little theoretical, let's end this chapter with a case study rooted in the practical world of one of the toughest relationships in business, a non-branded supplier to a major UK grocery multiple. It is a case that illustrates the journey of one such supplier towards a value machine, and in the process raising their supplier status from 'worried and ordinary' to 'strategic star'.

Next time you buy a loaf of wonderfully hot bread from a grocery store, you might pause to think of what was involved in getting it to you, and why. The bread was almost certainly only partly baked on the premises – most likely it was produced from a pre-baked loaf delivered to the supermarket by the supplier at the heart of this case.

The supplier had often been surprised at the arm's-length relationships they had with their customers, considering the value that they brought to the table. The margins made on their product were significantly higher than those made on bread sold off the shelf, sometimes by a factor of 10, and yet the customer was always reluctant to praise them, indeed seemed overly fond of chastising them. It was a mystery to the sales team.

Then one day they gathered together a deliberately cross-functional business team to produce a shared future analysis. It was then that the arguments began.

'Valuable?' said the man from the plant. 'Have you stopped to consider what it costs them to produce that bread?'

There was indeed the matter of the machinery required, and the staff, and most damning of all, the space. Once that was all taken into account the bread selling off the shelf suddenly seemed a rather more attractive proposition.

'But we're more valuable than that,' said a junior member of the team, who happened to spend more time in supermarkets than most of the senior managers sat around the table put together, 'I'm a shopper, and I should know. We help them make the place smell nice.'

Once the cynical laughter had subsided the MD stood up and walked over to the flipchart on which they had been creating their shared future analysis.

'What was it that we said they were trying to do? Build their brands through unique consumer propositions. And what was it we said frustrated them more than anything else? The problem of replicating in some of their smaller stores the theatre and performance they can achieve in their superstores. Don't you see, we're barking up the wrong tree.'

'How so?' asked the sales director, 'Don't margins like the ones we give them matter all of a sudden?'

Perhaps it was with just a little too much undisguised glee in their voice that the head of marketing responded: 'But we've already established that those margins soon disappear with all the extra costs.'

'Quite,' said the MD, 'that's not what they want from us – I'd even bet they would be happy to sell at no margin at all if they got what they really wanted.'

'And what's that?' said the sales director, appearing not to want to hear the answer.

'To help them replicate their in-store bakery in smaller stores.'

It was one of those moments, when everyone knew this was right, but nobody seemed to know how it could be done – they were back where they had started.

Then the lady from R&D started to speak, very quietly as she usually did so that normally most of what she said was never heard and she would retreat back into her shell, only this time the room was pin-droppingly quiet, and everyone was listening.

'You're right,' she began, 'if we could give them a product that required smaller ovens to bake it, and was easier to use so they didn't require so many staff, and perhaps if we helped them with training those staff…'

'Then everyone could have the same great smell!' chipped in the junior member of the team.

'But can we do that?' asked the MD.

All heads turned to the lady from the plant:

'Why not? We're doing it all the time in our lab...'

It had been a useful meeting, and just in case you think I might have a downer on sales people, it was the sales director who seized the baton of the new strategy. It wasn't about margins, it was about the customer's brand, and if they could develop products and services that helped the customer build a more uniform and consistent brand then their status as a key supplier was assured.

Part II

Targeting

4

Market segmentation

With targeting, everything starts with segmentation.

We aim to develop different working practices with different customer groups – some will be transactional, others might move towards collaborative partnerships – based on the returns we can get from them. Some form of customer classification will be required – segmentation is a good place to start.

We wish to match the capabilities of our organization with the true needs of our customers, but unless we are going to divide up our organization into individual customer-sized pieces we need to gather those customers into accessible working groups – segmentation is a good place to start.

We wish to maximize the benefits to ourselves of making such successful matches, so it would be good to replicate those successes across a number of like-minded customers – segmentation is a good place to start.

Not only is it a good place to start, segmentation is a foundation of sustainable competitive advantage. Products don't win you competitive advantage on their own. Imagine you have produced a wristwatch, the world's best wristwatch, so good it does everything imaginable from telling the time to navigating the stars, and as well as providing a valuable investment as a piece of jewellery, it's fun, a great gift, the height of fashion, a versatile accessory to any outfit, the ultimate badge of status, and keeps good time a thousand feet below the surface of the sea. So to whom are you going to sell this miracle wristwatch – everyone? If so we will have a problem – how much to charge?

You might be able to sell this watch as a navigation device for £250, as a piece of jewellery you might get £500, and as a badge of status perhaps over £1,000, but simply as a means of telling the time, only £30. In an open market (that is, with no segmentation strategy in place) the lowest common denominator will always win through – £30 for the most incredible watch ever invented.

It's not the product that determines your value; it's to whom you sell it, and how. Picture a small boy standing outside a greengrocer shop, looking at the price of apples. At one end of the window there are apples selling for £1 a kilo, while at the other the price tag says £2.50 a kilo. Puzzled, he goes inside to ask what is the difference – it must be something special. 'You're right,' replies the greengrocer, 'it's something very special indeed; the apples for £2.50 a kilo are there for people who *want* to pay £2.50 a kilo.'

That's OK for consumers, you might say, easily influenced by the tricks of marketing professionals (and greengrocers), but what about those tough-minded buyers in our B2B customers? Well, do you get premium prices from some of those buyers and not from others? Do some of them appreciate your value while others treat you as a commodity? Do some appear to want to pay more, because of how they perceive what they are getting? That's because some of them are in one segment, and the others in another – it's just to be hoped that you planned it that way.

This is the beauty of segmentation; it can bring you competitive advantage almost as the result of an intellectual exercise – and it comes for free.

And yet many businesses still run scared of segmentation, because it involves tough choices, and choices made tougher by the seemingly endless possibilities and options. So what if you make the wrong choice? Might it have been better not to have chosen in the first place? Some seem to think so... or they compromise with a half-hearted kind of segmentation that satisfies nobody.

Here's an example of what I mean. A manufacturer of lactose divides its market into four segments: 'pharmaceuticals', 'fast-moving consumer goods', 'dairy' and 'others'. For a start, what on earth is 'others'? As for the rest, how does this help? Are the needs of all dairy companies the same? Are the value propositions to be put to all pharmaceutical companies the same? What if a dairy company also regards itself as a manufacturer of fast-moving consumer goods? I would doubt that this segmentation has brought very much value to the supplier, and nor has it made much of an impact on the customer – so what was the point?

Feeling guilty? Many do when it comes to segmentation, particularly when they see the gulf between their practice and the definitions in the business textbooks. How many times have I seen newly qualified MBAs shuddering at what they find in their first employer after graduation? (By the time they move on to their second employer they have either forgotten their lessons or grown cynical about the whole matter…)

The definition is clear: a segment is a group of customers who share common needs, attitudes and behaviours. Building on that: as a result of their commonality they can be offered a common value proposition.

Manufacturers who focus on end consumers seem to have less of a problem with this definition. Table 4.1 illustrates an example of 'lifestyle segmentation', a hugely popular methodology in recent times used by suppliers in such diverse markets as food, clothing, cosmetics and household furnishings (the per cent of population in this example is for the UK).

Table 4.1 _Lifestyle segmentation_

Lifestyle	Description	% of pop
Self-explorers	Self-expression and self-realization, reject doctrine in favour of individual awareness, 'spiritual'.	15
Social resisters	Caring and altruistic, concerned for society and the environment, can be intolerant.	14
Experimentalists	Highly individual, fast-paced enjoyment, materialistic, pro-technology, anti-authority.	11
Conspicuous consumers	Acquisitive and competitive, concerned with position and show. Pro-authority and hierarchy.	19
Belongers	Conventional, traditional, seeking to fit in. Family orientated and resistant to change.	18
Survivors	Class conscious and community spirited. Aiming to 'get by'. Hardworking and apparently happy with their lot.	17
Aimless	a) young, unemployed, seeking 'kicks', anti-authority b) old, focused on day-to-day existence in trying circumstances.	5

Taken from _Marketing, an introductory text_ by M Christopher and M McDonald

It is easy to be cynical about any such listing, regarding it as oversimplified and artificial, particularly when taken out of context. We might question any basis of segmentation that puts a 17-year-old unemployed seeker of 'kicks' in the same segment as an elderly couple living on a meagre pension. Is a possible explanation that this 5 per cent of the population is what marketing people might consider a poor prospect, an 'underclass', unworthy of their further consideration? Perhaps, but the simple truth is, such approaches work; meaning: they result in clearer and more easily communicated value propositions, better distribution, better margins and higher profitability.

THE B2B CHALLENGE

It is when we turn to the world of B2B (business to business) that the problems seem to begin. The methodologies used by the world of fast-moving consumer goods don't always transfer that easily, and in the vast majority of cases, after a fleeting effort to mimic them, B2B suppliers resort to more traditional methods, dividing up their markets into industry types (as with the lactose supplier) or technical applications.

So, on behalf of our lactose supplier we must ask again the same question: do all pharmaceutical companies share the same needs, attitudes and behaviours? Rarely, if ever. If industry type doesn't help, the supplier might go to the next level of segmentation – applications – and segment perhaps by drug type, or by whether their product is used in the drugs 'active' (the vital ingredients) or in the 'delivery system' (the coating on the pill). This is certainly better, as it is more likely to highlight specific needs, attitudes and behaviours, but it is still unlikely that these are shared across different customers, at least not beyond some very basic technical issues.

Some, in desperation of the whole thing, resort to the 'ultimate solution' – 'we practice Key Account Management, each of those Key Accounts is a segment in their own right – and don't tell me that they don't each have unique needs, attitudes and behaviours!' Where a supplier has a very small number of individual customers such an approach may work – every customer is 'Key' – but what happens when there are thousands of customers? After the 'blessed few' are raised to the level of Key, the remainder can all too often be consigned to that graveyard of segmentation – 'others'.

Figure 4.1 indicates some different 'levels' of segmentation. How far do you go?

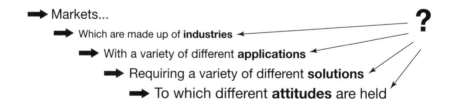

Figure 4.1 Levels of segmentation

Good segmentation is such an important part of a successful value machine that it is worth the effort to explore as far down the levels as possible – the suggestion being that the further down you manage to go the greater your chance of finding sustainable competitive advantage.

SEGMENTING BY SOLUTION, OR VALUE RECEIVED

Use whatever words suit your own circumstance, and don't worry about landing outside these simple definitions. Segmenting by *solution* type might mean customer groupings that use different technologies, or are seeking different levels of value, or have different levels of investment that they are prepared to make in order to receive that value. This sounds rather like segmenting by customer *attitudes* – some might call this segmenting by *value received*.

Let's consider the case of a supplier who made the effort to go beyond the norm. They are a manufacturer of automated GPS-assisted line painting equipment – that is to say, clever machines that will get on with painting the lines on a football pitch without a man pushing a cart full of paint. They are at the leading edge of their market, it being fair to say that most customers still make do with 'Bert and the cart'. In launching a new line of equipment, which was far from cheap, they had to consider a new strategy – adverts in the normal trade press were not going to work…

They made use of a technique for market segmentation much favoured by FMCG (fast-moving consumer goods) companies sometimes referred to as 'psychographics', perhaps better described as being a means of identifying different values received by different customers.

The key question asked is: what will the customer do with this product and how will they get value from doing that? Three potential answers are illustrated in Figure 4.2, where the size of the circle represents the envisaged size of the market measured by units sold.

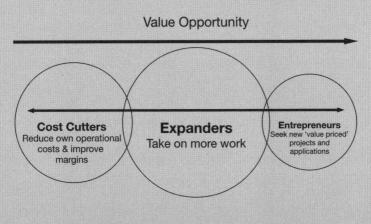

Value Opportunity

Cost Cutters
Reduce own operational costs & improve margins

Expanders
Take on more work

Entrepreneurs
Seek new 'value priced' projects and applications

Figure 4.2 *Segmentation by value received*

The *cost cutters* were customers who would use the machine to reduce their own operational costs – they would make Bert redundant. The *expanders* would use the machine to take on more business of the same type. The *entrepreneurs* would use the machine to develop new applications with their customers; instead of merely painting lines on the football field perhaps they could also paint the club crest in the centre circle?

The value to the supplier of this exercise was enormous. All at once they realized that they needed three variants of the new machine – the cost cutters would only want the most basic model, no frills, and at a knock-down price. The expanders would be interested in features that would allow them to monitor usage, so helping them to forecast future demands and plan more work (not to mention buy new machines). The entrepreneurs would want the full specification…

Once that was realized, questions of profitability arose. The nature of the supplier's business was not based on volume and economies of scale; these were expensive specialist pieces of equipment even at the 'knock-down price' end of the market. Value pricing, that is, pricing based on the level of value received, meant that the more ambitious products were likely to be the most profitable, and this resulted in a redrawing of the segmentation model, with the circles now representing the profit to be had from each segment, as shown in Figure 4.3.

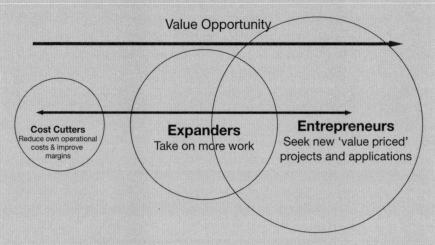

Figure 4.3 *Segmentation and profitability*

From that point it became clear that they should focus their attentions on the full specification model for the entrepreneur segment. The nature of the investment required was clear, as was the level of return on that investment, and all functions could proceed with their best efforts, by their own functional standards, knowing that they were contributing to the overall success of the business strategy.

THE NESTING CONCEPT

B2B suppliers struggling with the concept of segmenting by customer attitudes rather than industry types or applications might find help in the 'nesting' concept, developed by Benson P Shapiro and Thomas V Bonoma. This aims to help a supplier work through the complexity and range of criteria by considering a hierarchy of choices, as shown in Figure 4.4.

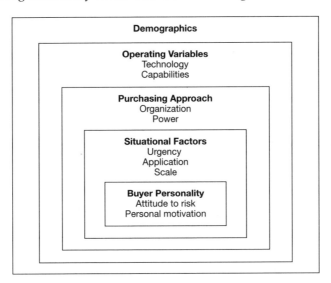

Figure 4.4   *The nesting concept*
From BP Shapiro and TV Bonoma, *Harvard Business Review*, May–June 1984

The model suggests that demographics provides the starting point, and the most basic criteria on which to segment, but that within that are four further levels, of increasing specificity. First come the operating variables, such as the client's technology, their capabilities, their use of products and brands. The nest within that nest looks at purchasing approaches – the way that clients buy. Next come the situational factors – the product application, the urgency, the scale. Finally comes the buyer personality; their attitude to risk, their motivation and so on.

Similar to the comment made regarding the *levels of segmentation* (see Figure 4.1), the general observation can be made that the closer to the central nest you get in segmenting the market the more likely you are to find a source of sustainable competitive advantage. The price you pay? It just takes more thought.

A fertiliser manufacturer found their product to be in slow decline in a mature market. They decided to segment as a means to finding new offers, testing first the more obvious 'cuts'; crop type, soil type, climate type, seasonality and so on. Finally they hit on a simple truth – wheat never rang in an order, nor did light loamy soil… it was farmers every time!

Farmers came from different backgrounds, with widely differing attitudes, aspirations and buying behaviours. Once the manufacturer started to explore these factors they began to understand (almost for the first time) what *really* made people buy their product, or not. The final segmentation was done by personal and business profiles, looking at attitudes and needs: the traditional family farmer being found to have a rather different outlook to the graduate of agricultural college managing a large estate.

Division of the market into six segments, illustrated in Figure 4.5, allowed the business to prioritize their attentions on those that would respond best to the business's own strengths. The resultant matching of capabilities to needs meant greater focus, a more targeted range of value propositions, more relevant value for the customer, and significant improvement to the supplier's own operational structure. All of this resulted in greater customer satisfaction, greater supplier profitability, and progress towards a true value machine.

Figure 4.5 *Segmentation by personal/business profiles*

NOVEL SEGMENTATION

There are always many ways to slice the cake. Novel methods of segmentation can often be the best simply because they are unique to you – and that way lies competitive advantage. The following case illustrates a successful approach in a particularly complex B2B environment using _time_ as its basis.

A supplier of molecules to the pharmaceutical industry had segmented for some while by therapeutic area; there was an asthma segment, an allergy segment, a cancer segment, an osteoporosis segment, indeed there was a segment for each and every malady treatable. This really did very little for them as not only did every one of their competitors do the same, but they found the behaviour and attitudes of separate customers to be quite different even in the same segment. What they found (from hard-won experience) was that it wasn't the therapeutic area that determined customer behaviour but the phase of development that the drug was at.

A drug must pass through a series of checkpoints on its way from research to market, including efficacy tests, trials, and regulatory approvals, and these fall into four distinct phases. A pharmaceutical company will have rather different concerns and needs moving from one phase to the next, but they are quite precise and uniform within a single phase, providing an excellent opportunity for segmentation for the observant supplier.

At the first phase of development the pharmaceutical companies want speed and flexibility from their suppliers, with price and quality some long way down the list. It doesn't matter if the drug doesn't work perfectly – these are early days about establishing potential, and fast. As the development proceeds through the phases their interests change towards ever-greater quality and reliability, and then to an absolute ability to gain regulatory approval. Once that is achieved the interests turn to matters of scaling up and the control or reduction of production costs.

The molecule supplier were able to identify these phases as discrete segments, developing graded offers that met the different needs, attitudes and behaviours, almost regardless of drug type.

Perhaps the most significant aspect of this novel segmentation was the way in which it freed the supplier's functions from some unnecessary straitjackets. Working to the earlier 'drug type' model each function was obliged to work to what might be thought of as 'Rolls Royce standards' on all occasions (for those who think this to be a good general discipline, just think of the cost, the excess, the waste, the time...). The new segmentation allowed functions to come to more intelligent decisions as to what standards were required. It wasn't a licence to be sloppy; it was licence to be appropriate.

FOCUSING THE EFFORTS

Almost whatever your method of segmentation there always seem to be more segments available than you can deal with – which is no bad thing. So we have two questions: what methodology; and which final target segments to choose?

Once again we find an important role for the leadership team – not necessarily in making the final choice (those closer to the action are often better placed) but in establishing the criteria for that choice. The role of the leadership team is to keep the following questions in the minds of those choosing the methodology for segmentation:

- How will this help us to focus our resources on a genuine understanding of customer needs, ambitions and worries?
- How will this help us match our capabilities to those needs, ambitions and worries?
- How will this help us facilitate the creation of unique value propositions?
- How will this help us to align functions behind a common strategy and approach?
- How will this help us to be more efficient, more effective and more profitable?
- How will this benefit the customer?
- How will this help us to build the value machine?

Once the methodology is decided and the range of specific segment options is before us, a common approach in the final selection of prime targets is to use a *directional policy matrix*, as shown in Figure 4.6.

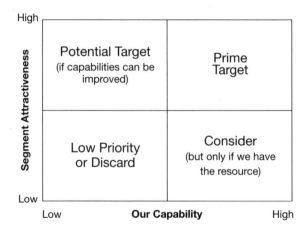

Figure 4.6 *The Directional Policy Matrix (DPM)*

The DPM maps the segment options on the vertical axis ranked in order of attractiveness. Use a consistent set of attractiveness criteria, perhaps including a selection from the following: size, profit opportunity, growth, ease of access, readiness to adopt, attitudes to value, level of competition, or whatever else spells attractive in your business environment.

The options are also mapped on the horizontal axis ranked by our level of capability, which might include the following kinds of issue: resources, capacity, budget, ability to tailor, technology, patents, brands, service package, etc.

It isn't as simple as saying that those in the top right – the prime targets – are the only ones to chase; that would be to risk consigning your business to history, the history of your own capabilities. Perhaps there is a need to develop those capabilities, in pursuit of a better match with attractive segments? In other words, to convert the potential targets into prime targets through self-improvement.

It's a typical enough choice: go for what you can, or stretch your ambitions and go for what is truly most attractive? There are plenty of competing investment and return considerations, but suffice it to say that true value machines usually aim to stretch their ambitions – self-improvement in pursuit of attractive business is part of the credo.

5

Customer classification

If you have not yet conducted a rigorous segmentation of your market, or do not yet have agreement on the prime and potential target segments (see Chapter 4) then be doubly patient before leaping too quickly into matters of customer classification. What if you were to classify a customer as a 'Key Account' only to find it part of an unattractive or low priority segment? It may well be a large customer (Key Accounts often are) but might it be one that represents your past rather than your future?

There are three mortal sins of customer classification:

1. Rushing too fast to label customers before having got the foundations of segmentation agreed (by all functions) and in place.
2. Pushing too many customers into the Key Account classification.
3. *'Sizeism'* – the sin of thinking the biggest are the most important.

Chapter 4 aimed to help avoid the first sin, this chapter will deal with the remaining two, and go on to suggest a method for classification proven to help build an effective value machine.

A recent survey into the nature and sophistication of Key Account Management (KAM) practice in Scandinavia made some interesting discoveries. Suppliers are good at managing their largest customers. They have good processes in place, clear management understanding of the task, and a level of skill in the KA teams that matches any in the world, but there are still problems.

KAM is found to be largely in the hands of sales people – a short-term, sales-driven process. The task of KAM is well understood by senior management, but their support is lacking when it's needed the most – Key Account Managers lack sufficient authority and the internal functions don't always 'play ball'. But most revealingly, and most worryingly, the single most important criterion for identifying a supplier's Key Accounts is size.

Such observations are not limited to Scandinavia by any means, indeed the Swedes the Danes and the Norwegians are probably more advanced in the 'good practices' of KAM than most, not least in recognizing the requirements for improvement.

It seems that KAM has become identified with big customers, and while it is to be welcomed that efficient and effective processes for managing such customers have been developed, it should be said that true KAM is something rather more important than this – KAM is about managing your future.

Before developing this point let's deal with the perils of _sizeism_, that is, ranking your customers by their revenue, and so determining that your Key Accounts are simply the largest.

THE PERILS OF SIZEISM

Consider why your largest customers are the largest; it's all down to the past. History has got them to where they are, and as they say in the advertisements for investment products: 'past performance should not be taken as a guarantee of future potential'.

Wouldn't it worry you if an outsider, knowing nothing of your business, could identify your Key Accounts simply by looking at your sales statistics? It should worry you sick.

Base your assessments of importance on size alone and it won't be long before your big customers know it, and start demanding the kind of 'attentions' that their size so clearly warrants.

Focus on size, chase size, champion size, and you'll end up with big customers, perhaps at the cost of those medium or small customers who may bring a host of important benefits such as a greater desire to partner, more dynamic growth ambitions, or simply better margins.

Build your business around the largest customers and you grow dependent upon them – someone has to fill those factories that you built, and don't they just know it…

Of course, if you have a business that benefits from economies of scale then big orders from big customers will be very important, but even then, does that make such a customer a Key Account, or just a big account?

Will everyone in the business agree with a disproportionate attention to the largest customers? It is quite typical to hear complaints from the folk in R&D, manufacturing, logistics, finance, and customer service, along the following lines: 'They're *too* big. They bully us. The sales people let them get away with murder. They must be losing us money…' Don't expect too much enthusiasm for cross-functional alignment where such thoughts abound.

It is very likely that the largest customers are not the most profitable, and for all the obvious reasons: they win the biggest discounts, they have the best payment terms, and they get the largest share of our attention and services (probably for free). Unfortunately, as most suppliers fail to measure customer profitability with any real accuracy, they remain blissfully unaware of the likely truth. Given that the company makes decent profits overall, they might argue, then surely at least some of our big customers must be making good money for us? It's rather as Henry Ford once observed when considering the huge advertising spend of his company: 'Half of what we spend on advertising' he said, 'is effective. The trouble is, we don't know which half.' Would you go out of your way to devote even more of your valuable time and resources on such a half-hearted act of faith?

Can a customer be too big? How would you feel (or sleep at nights) if just one customer accounted for more than half of your business? Sure this would make such a customer 'Key', but must you get yourself into such a perilous position in the first place? I know of several very successful (and highly profitable) companies that lay down rules about such things. One that always makes me smile has an upper limit for any customer of 15 per cent of their turnover, and has often turned down offers of more business that would break the rule. Interestingly their customers understood the reasons and respect them – and relationships thrive.

Do big customers make the safest investments? Survival of the biggest has never been much of a theory – if it had been, we would still have the dinosaurs…

Of all the sins of *sizeism*, the one likely to be most damaging to the prospect of a strong and effective value machine is that of misdirected resources and effort. How does the following 'logic' sound to you?:

1. The value machine aims to match a supplier's best resources to those customers promising the best future returns on that investment…
2. A supplier's largest customers tend to receive the best attention from the supplier's best people – usually the lion's share of the resources in both quantity and quality…

3. If the best future returns are expected from the largest customers then no problem – the matching process is sorted – but is this necessarily so?
4. 'Best returns', in a value machine context, should be defined more broadly than the size of the revenue. What about the prospect of working in collaborative partnership with a customer? What about the prospect of learning from the experience, to the benefit of all customers? What about the prospect of developing new value propositions that enhance the supplier's capabilities?
5. Might some of those kinds of returns come from customers other than the largest?

KEY ACCOUNTS – OUR MOST IMPORTANT INVESTMENTS

Here is the argument in essence: view your customers as investments, have a broad definition of what makes a 'good return', and the list of Key Accounts might look rather different.

As we have noted, most KAM strategies have developed as a means of managing the biggest customers, which is not necessarily the same thing as managing a supplier's most important investments.

For a start, we will need to use different selection criteria in our _customer classification process_, and some of those criteria might seem alarmingly subjective – alarming that is to those used to making their choices through Excel spreadsheets.

Next, we will require a different investment strategy, allocating resources in a different (but still disproportionate) way.

Most telling of all, the contributions made by each function will be different. The rules of engagement will change from 'largest comes first' to 'the best investment comes first'. There is an obvious implication in this last statement: _everyone_ involved needs to understand the nature of the investments – how they are made, and how their returns are measured.

A vital question in any investment strategy is: how long? Just how far ahead do we look in determining what makes a good investment? Stretch the time horizon too far and we risk losing today's business as costs escalate and revenues stagnate. Go too short-term and we risk killing the value machine concept before it has chance to breath.

The business must look to its leadership team to judge the right balance between 'jam today' and 'jam tomorrow', but it can go further than that; it can make use of a customer classification process designed to deliver whatever the desired balance, and to stay flexible enough to cope when that balance has to change. Some customers will be classified as long-term investments (we might call them our *Development Key Accounts*), while others must provide money today (perhaps some of our *Key Accounts*, perhaps our *Maintenance Accounts?*). This is the language of the classification process outlined below.

A CLASSIFICATION PROCESS

Figure 5.1 lays out a six-step process designed to help navigate the way through what can be a bewildering mass of questions, analysis and debate, helping avoid the inevitable bear traps that lie in wait, and with the ultimate objective of a customer classification agreed by all functions. Cross-functional agreement is vital as this will allow each function to set its own rules of customer engagement in line with its own standards of functional excellence – a key requirement of the value machine.

Step 1. Objectives

Step 2. Market Segmentation

Step 3. Assemble the Classification and Selection team

Step 4. Classification – the 'K.A.I.S.M.'

    i. *Customer Attractiveness Factors*

    ii. *Relative Strength Factors*

Step 5. Customer Distinction

Step 6. Communication, Alignment and Implementation

Figure 5.1 *The six-step process*

Step 1. Objectives

The leadership team must be crystal clear about the purpose of the classification process. This is not a sales-driven exercise, but a business-wide strategy, designed to ensure the optimum allocation of resources to the best opportunities. The expected outcomes from this matching process should also be made clear – enhanced value propositions, better direct rewards from customers, and lower costs through more effective and efficient use of resources. In other words, the leadership team must fully articulate the philosophy of the value machine.

Step 2. Market segmentation

Chapter 4 dealt with this step, which must come before the process of customer classification itself. Just one reminder of why good segmentation is so important: an objective of any value machine must be to learn from customer interactions and apply that learning to other customers, so maximizing the return on what can be a significant initial investment. Good segmentation is one of the mechanisms by which this transfer of capability is enabled.

Step 3. Assemble the classification and selection team

This is, I confess, a tricky one: who, and how many, should be involved in these all-important decisions? I have watched a genuinely cross-functional team of over 20 well-intentioned managers sink into a bureaucratic bog of their own making from which no good decisions were ever going to arise. I have also looked on as a pair of self-assured (not to say arrogant) managers spent an hour on the task and parted company entirely happy with what was a crisp and concise conclusion. As I search for a moral to the tale, these two examples worry me. The intentions of the former were good – something went wrong in the execution. The precision of the latter was admirable, but how likely were they to carry anyone with them? (I happen to know that they didn't.)

There are people in your own organization who already know which customers are key, and people who know which will most likely make the best investments, and people who know which ones to maintain, and _can_ be maintained, with minimum effort. Trust me, these people exist; the problem is that they are not necessarily the same people in each case. And even if you do possess such an all-seeing, all-knowing individual, don't expect anyone else to give much heed to such a maverick. You may think me cynical, but I have watched organizations grapple with this problem for many years and the same issues arise time after time – people issues.

How many and how broad?

The answers to those two questions – who, and how many? – are to be found by first reminding ourselves of the objectives set in Step 1 of the process.

If our aim is to ensure that all functions subscribe to the classification, then that will guide our thinking. If we aim for more than this – to ensure a customer classification based on the best knowledge of all involved – then again that will guide our decision. If we wish to go one step further (and I hope you do), to ensure a classification that allows us to develop the most effective value propositions, of benefit to both customer and ourselves, then that will be yet further guide to our decision. That a team is necessary should be undisputed, but don't make it *too* large a one, however well intentioned. There is no need to have every last interest represented – a team of many more than six people will very likely start to hit problems. Aim for a team that represents those functions contributing most directly to the creation of customer value.

There are further questions that will guide us on how large or broad a team we might need. What is our current knowledge of our customers: good enough for such classifications? Do we have broad agreement as a business, or are there widely differing views between and across functions? Do we have a dynamic customer base, changing its nature and compensation with speed, or is it long-standing and stable? Finally, are we currently successful with existing methods of classification? You will see, I think, the purpose of these questions. If you have some of these problems then a broader base will be required, but if you don't have them, don't go looking for them through a complex of committees.

How senior… or how junior?

We gather a senior team who approach the task with their eyes on the long-term strategic objectives. 'Vision' abounds – which is great – but what do they know about the details of the customers? Why should the rest of the business accept their decisions if there is doubt over their knowledge of the details?

So we gather a team from sales and customer service, people with day-to-day experience of the customers, and their efforts reflect their intimate knowledge. 'Fine,' say the bosses, 'but what about tomorrow's customers? Where's the vision?' And why should the rest of the business accept these decisions any more easily if they think them the outcome of a mono-function perspective?

If I think of the more successful teams set up to tackle this problem, a few pieces of advice (and only that – these are neither rules nor instructions) might be hazarded. The best teams have been compact – and able to meet regularly without fear of absences or loss of interest. The best teams have not necessarily had all the 'customer expertise' on board, but they have been empowered to have access to such expertise through people outside the team. The best teams have been senior enough, or possess the authority of breadth and respected experience, for the business to take note of their conclusions. And finally, the best teams have proceeded through the detailed analysis with the help of a robust process, which brings us to Step 4.

Step 4. Classification – the K.A.I.S.M.

A, B, C, or perhaps Gold, Silver, Bronze; typical classifications used to indicate customer importance and priorities. Do they work? Probably not, as they fall foul of the sin of 'one-dimensionalism' (a term that I have just invented, but a sin that has been long in existence). This is the sin of thinking that you can classify your customers based solely on criteria of how attractive they are – Gold is more attractive than Silver, and so it goes on. Most businesses find this relatively easy, which is why most businesses do it…

Figure 5.2 shows the K.A.I.S.M. or Key Account Identification and Selection Matrix, a tool that adds an all-important second dimension to the process.

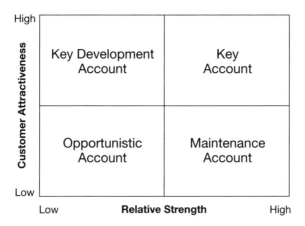

Figure 5.2 *The K.A.I.S.M*

The vertical axis ranks the attractiveness of the customer to us, while the horizontal axis ranks our attractiveness to the customers, what we will call 'our relative strength' when compared to our competitors. The ranking of the horizontal axis is our 'second dimension', and it isn't easy to do, which is why so many businesses skip this part…

The resulting matrix gives us four customer classifications:

1. *Key Accounts* are those where the attraction is mutual – we like the look of them and their future, and they rate us as a future supplier more strongly than they rate our competitors.
2. *Key Development Accounts* are those for which we would love to have big future plans, but who currently prefer one or more of our competitors (or perhaps simply don't know about us).
3. *Maintenance Accounts* are those that rate us highly, but we don't view as our most attractive future prospects.
4. *Opportunistic Accounts* are those where neither regards the other as of great future attraction (or if that sound too negative, how about 'where we are mutually neutral'?).

An important word, used in each definition, is 'future'. For the K.A.I.S.M. to be useful in the context of the value machine we need to remember that 'Key' customers are important investments. The criteria used to place the customers in this matrix should therefore aim to be future orientated wherever possible.

Given these definitions, and the realization that the K.A.I.S.M. is a tool for managing investments, we might start to look on certain customers in a new light. Which of them are in fact the 'most important'? Is it the *Key Accounts*, where we are already established and successful? Is it the *Key Development Accounts*, who might represent our future prosperity? Is it the *Maintenance Accounts*, who will provide us with the revenue and profit today to finance our ambitions elsewhere? This last classification may very well include some of those 'large' customers on which everyone has been focusing their attentions…

Each classification plays its part of course; even the *Opportunistic Accounts* have their role – somewhere to turn when the bosses want another 5 per cent growth before the end of the quarter. We are looking at a portfolio of accounts that will help us achieve that long-term short-term balance. We are also looking at a portfolio where each classification will require its own 'rules of engagement'. We will return to this idea in Step 5.

Attractiveness factors

There are many factors to consider, the following lists some of those most typically used:

- Size (yes, it *should* be on the list, provided it is not *alone* on the list!) – volume, value, profit.
- Growth potential – volume, value, profit.
- Financial stability.
- Ease of access – geography, openness, etc.
- Quality of existing relationships.
- Strategic fit – do they see the world the same way as we do? Will they take us where we wish to be?
- Are they 'early adopters' – do they pick up on new ideas and products, or do they wait until the market has tested them?
- Do they value our offer? Is it relevant to their needs?
- Level of competition (low being attractive).
- Their market standing – industry leader, credibility, prestige and so on…
- Will we learn from this customer – will they improve us?
- Will they collaborate on joint development projects?

Aim to make your choice as future orientated as possible, but of course include those current realities that are important to you – it is not particularly helpful to focus heavily on future potential if today you have a cash crisis and need current revenue to survive.

Aim to combine what we might call 'hard' or quantitative factors with 'soft' or qualitative factors (what some call the 'subjective' factors). Don't be scared of the 'soft' factors; too many years of hearing the mantra 'if you can't measure it you can't manage it' causes many to dismiss these things as irrelevant. They are far from that; they may just hold the secret of a successful classification process. One such soft factor that is clearly very important to the value machine philosophy is: will we learn from this customer – do they improve us?

In working the process you will be wise to list as many factors as possible at first, to be sure of not missing anything (the first 10 that come into your mind are the 'standard' criteria, and it is in the realm of the 'non-standard' that the 'golden nuggets' are often to be found), and then boil those factors down to a list of between four and eight – six is often considered 'ideal'.

We restrict the number of factors for two reasons: the K.A.I.S.M. process is a mathematical one – the more factors, the more the outcome is blurred, but more importantly, this is a process that you want the whole business to understand and follow – too many factors will simply lead to confusion.

One last point on the attractiveness factors – and you will see now another reason why segmentation must come first – all the customers in any given segment can be measured against a common list of factors, but change the segment, and the attractiveness factors might need to change. This means that the K.A.I.S.M. process should be repeated for each segment under consideration.

Relative strength factors

The identification of the factors for the vertical axis – 'their attraction to us' – is reasonably straightforward for two reasons:

1. You are in control of them – they relate to your own objectives and aspirations.
2. They will be the same for all customers in any given market segment.

The factors on the horizontal axis are rather harder to identify because here we need to view the world through the customer's eyes. What are _their_ objectives and aspirations, and how does that translate into their rating of suppliers? Hard stuff to access, but so hugely valuable to know.

Not only are these factors harder to identify and rate, they will also be different for each customer. Some customers publish explicit lists of vendor ratings while others are more secretive. Some will use 'hard' measures, others will favour more subjective evaluations based on perceptions rather than facts. Don't expect a ranking to the same precision as the vertical axis – we will of course be expressing views and opinions to a much greater extent.

In Chapter 8 we will examine an increasingly standard process by which purchasing professionals rate and position their suppliers (see Figure 8.6). In many ways it is the mirror image of the K.A.I.S.M. – a four-box-matrix process for classifying suppliers – and so an understanding of the customer's analysis will provide us with many important clues to our relative strengths, but there is a health warning: always remember that the professional buyer's view is only one of many in the customer's organization. This is often just as well and a 'good thing', as we will see in Chapter 7 when discussing the customer's decision-making processes, but it certainly adds to the complexity of completing this horizontal axis.

Identifying these factors will require great honesty. It is tempting to select all those things that you just happen to be good at, and you will feel very pleased with the outcome, only it will be worthless. The perceptions of the different functions within your own business will be of great value to this debate – each will have their own awareness of what goes down well and what causes complaints.

There are those people in any business who tend to pat themselves on the back with naive optimism when assessing the customers' views, just as there are those that whip themselves unreasonably. We don't want our analysis to succumb to either extreme (and nor is a compromise down the middle any more helpful), so it may be valuable to gain some kind of independent insight as a route to the truth in this matter. Consider formal and independent market research into customers' views, needs and levels of satisfaction. Using research as a way of talking to customers will be a good antidote to one of many a supplier's greatest failings – talking to themselves.

The range of factors (seen from your customers' perspective) might include any of the following:

- price;
- service – on time in full measures, just-in-time requirements, etc;
- quality;
- speed of response;
- relationships and attitudes;
- technical innovation;
- investment in the industry;
- value in use – value in the supply chain, total acquisition cost, etc;
- attitude to exclusivity arrangements;
- long-term sustainability;
- trust and confidence – ethical standards and behaviour;
- level of risk (see Chapter 8 for more on this factor).

Completing the analysis

There are software packages available to help complete the process but it is no bad idea to commence with a paper exercise, however rough, and for several reasons: it quickly identifies the black holes in your knowledge of your customers; it makes a team-wide analysis easier to facilitate; and most importantly, it engages the brain rather than your typing fingers.

The two tables shown in Figures 5.3 and 5.4 are designed to help you identify where your customers sit in your portfolio – recording your scores for the vertical axis (Figure 5.3) and the horizontal axis (Figure 5.4).

	Account/Customer	Customer Attractiveness Factor (CAF) Scores						
		CAF 1	CAF 2	CAF 3	CAF 4	CAF 5	CAF 6	Total Score
1								
2								
3								
4								
5								
6								
7								
8								
9								
10								
11								
12								

Figure 5.3 _Customer attractiveness factors_

- Enter your chosen customers across the top of the table.
- Enter the attractiveness factors.
- Enter a score from 1 to 10 for each customer, against each attractiveness factor. The higher the score, the better your customer meets that aspiration. Try to set a benchmark of what is 'good and bad' before starting to score, and try to stick to it! (It is all too easy to upgrade your 'favourite' customers.)
- Calculate the average score (the grand total of all the total scores divided by the number of customers assessed).

		Customer/Account..					
		Relative Strength Factor (RSF) Scores					
	Relative Strength Factors	Weight %	Your Own Business	Comp 1	Comp 2	Comp 3	Comp 4	Comp 5
1								
2								
3								
4								
5								
6								
	Total Score:	(100%)						

Figure 5.4 *Relative strength factors*

- For each customer under consideration, identify six relative strength factors (RSFs) that represent their principal needs from their suppliers and the criteria by which they would judge you in comparison with others.
- Complete one table for each of the customers selected for analysis, it being quite likely that each customer will have their own distinct set of RSFs.
- Place you and your competitors across the top of the table and enter a score from 1 to 10 for each supplier, against each factor. This is how the customer views you and your competitors, fact and perception – so be honest! The higher the score, the better the supplier meets the customer's criteria.

These tables will help you to prepare a 'first cut' analysis, but you may wish to go further than this. Weighting of individual factors is the obvious next step and if you want to take the mathematics that far then it is at this point that you should turn to a software package – the sums start to get quite involved!

Completing the matrix

Using the information from these two tables, you can place each customer on the K.A.I.S.M. (Figure 5.2).

From the customer attractiveness factors table shown in Figure 5.3, if a customer scores higher than the average score then they will be in one of the two upper boxes; if lower than average, they will be in one of the two lower boxes.

To identify which of the lower two, use the results from the relative strength factors table shown in Figure 5.4. Where you score better than your best competitor you will occupy the right-hand box, but the left-hand box if you score worse.

Mathematics or debate?

This is an exercise that lends itself to all sorts of sophisticated mathematical treatments, but for myself, I confess to preferring to leave the maths to one side.

Given that you probably already have a fair idea of which customer is going to appear in what box without reaching for a pocket calculator, it is important to note that the most important part of this process is very often not the outcome, but the debate that gets you there. By involving a broad team in the process it can become a 'persuasive process', an important part of getting everyone across the business to act on the results (see Step 5).

The debate doesn't finish once the four-box matrix has been produced. Once people see the 'circles in the boxes' don't be surprised if a whole lot of new factors come tumbling out, and particularly those 'soft' ones, as people start to argue about the relative customer placings. Regard this part of the debate as good news, as it will very likely be at this point, by re-engaging the brain as opposed to being ruled by mathematics, that the best results occur.

The 'hard' factors will have looked at such things as size, market share, growth, revenue and profitability. But there is more to life than this. How about the fact that they like you, or not? How about the fact that they are in bed with the competition, or not? How about the fact that their business is absolutely ideal for those who have to run your plant, or those who have to manage the logistical operations, or not? And so it goes on.

An option, and a quite workable one, is to do the maths first, on sets of 'hard' factors, and then build in the 'soft' factors later, through debate. This may result in the shifting of customers, as shown in Figure 5.5.

This isn't about cheating (promoting your favourite customers by post-rationalization); it is about taking note of opinions, and recognizing that such classifications are subject to a complex range of influences.

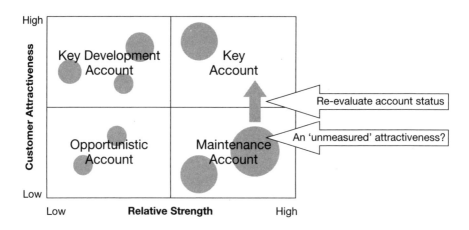

Figure 5.5 *Re-engaging the brain...*

How many KAs and KDAs?

Before turning to Step 5 we have two last questions: how many *Key Accounts*, and how many *Key Development Accounts* should we have?

Regarding the *Key Accounts* the answer is: as few as possible. This may seem a strange comment – wouldn't you want lots of customers that are attractive to you and where you are attractive to them? You may want them, but can you manage them? In Chapter 6 we will look at the requirements of KAM, and at that point the number comes tumbling down. In the vast majority of cases counting them on the fingers of two hands should represent the maximum, and if it is a business new to KAM, make it one hand.

Surely then we should want lots of *Key Development Accounts*, so guaranteeing a great future? Again we should recognize the nature of the task. These are customers that will need significant efforts to 'convert' and then work alongside. They will take a large slice of our resources (see Step 5, and Figure 5.6 below). They will need 'courting' or 'wooing', and we all know the effort involved in that activity in our private lives; it is a useful analogy to consider with customers in the top left box. It is almost always better to focus one's efforts in this regard; better to be brilliant on two or three occasions than mediocre on 20 (and at this point I hope my analogy breaks down...).

There may be a better way of asking the question – how many should we have? – and that is: how many do we *need*? This takes us right to the heart of the value machine philosophy. If we regard our most important customers as our most important investments, and if the purpose of those investments is to improve our own business through a better matching of capabilities and resources to customer needs, then we can reasonably ask: how many such investments do we *need* in order to improve our business?

If we have segmented our market, so that each segment contains customers with similar needs, attitudes and behaviours, then doesn't the act of improving ourselves for one customer in that segment improve us for all? Once again, because it is a point worth repeating, isn't it better to be brilliant on just a few occasions than mediocre on many?

Step 5. Customer distinction

Having classified our customer under four broad headings (Key Accounts, Key Development Accounts, Maintenance Accounts, Opportunistic Accounts) we must now determine the means to distinguish between them.

How will our approach to each of the four classes differ? How will we apply our resources in each case? How should we aim to manage each class of customer? Will we have different contractual arrangements, different service packages, and might even our prices and our terms be different?

Differential resourcing

In broad terms we are speaking of _differential resourcing,_ largely a question of where we spend our time and our money, as illustrated in Figure 5.6.

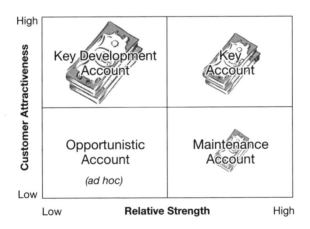

Figure 5.6 _Differential resourcing_

If we were to end up with no distinction between the four customer types, then, and quite apart from having wasted our time entirely, we would be committing three further sins, at the very least.

Sin number one: we make it impossible for those involved in servicing the customers to decide how to act, other than to give everyone the same, or to decide on their own prioritization. This would be a direct contradiction of everything the value machine is meant to be.

Sin number two: we will suffer from 'service creep'. Perhaps for an initial period, despite our failure to lay down lines of distinction, the Key Accounts will get the best attention, the best ideas, the best services, indeed the best of everything, but it won't be long before jealous eyes from those involved with non Key Accounts start to want the same things for their customers. Soon everyone has what was once exclusive to the Key Accounts; so what was the point of setting them apart? It gets worse; it is very likely that the return on these non Key Account investments will be less (and if they are not, then there was something wrong with your initial classification!). And worse yet, the level of complexity with which you now burden your business might be fatal. Again, this would be a direct contradiction of everything the value machine is meant to be.

Sin number three: by not finding ways of reducing time and effort to *Maintenance* and *Opportunistic Accounts*, you will never free up enough time and energy to allow a proper practice of KAM with the *Key* and *Key Development Accounts*. It is an irony that for many businesses the real challenge of KAM is not to be found in the management of the Key and Key Development Accounts, but in finding new ways to look after those customers defined otherwise!

Figure 5.7 illustrates the idea of 'freeing up the energy'. It also indicates, very broadly, the nature and purpose of the relationship management task with each customer class. These terms – *hunting, farming* and *harvesting* – will be explored further in Chapter 6.

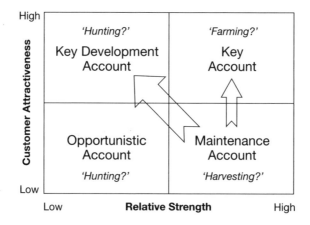

Figure 5.7 *Freeing up the energy...*

The 'bases' of customer distinction

Figure 5.7 illustrates how for the value machine to operate effectively energy and resources must be liberated from those customers 'below the line' on the K.A.I.S.M. and applied 'above the line'. To do this, distinct relationship and service strategies must be developed for each customer type. These strategies are likely to impact on all functions within the business – it will form their 'rules of engagement'.

The following list gives just some of the possible 'bases' for customer distinction:

- expectation of R.O.I. (return on investment) – profitability and the time horizon;
- frequency of contact;
- deployment of a team (or not);
- level and depth of contacts;
- involvement of senior management;
- nature of commitment to the customer;
- contracts – _long or short, or none at all_;
- allocation of resources;
- access to resources;
- availability of technology;
- commercial or technical 'openness';
- nature and number of projects;
- provision of services;
- charging for services, or part of the package?
- terms and pricing;
- scope and detail of the Account Plan;
- direct supply or use of distributors;
- how the customer views us…

The task, once you have selected your bases, is to determine how each base would manifest itself for each customer classification. Try to define applications or expectations across a 'minimum and a maximum' range in each case.

If, for instance, the base was _level and depth of contact_, then in the case of a Key Account you might require contact with the customer's CEO, or at least with the functional directors or vice-presidents. For an Opportunistic Account the level required might go no higher than the person who places the order.

Regarding the timing of our return on investment we would perhaps grant the longest payback time to work done with Key Development Accounts whereas returns should be immediate from Opportunistic Accounts and pretty much immediate from Maintenance Accounts, and 'fairly fast' (but try to be more precise than that!) from Key Accounts, given our established position.

Table 5.1 shows an example in summary form of the finished result. Please note that it is only that, an example; there is no obligation to copy any issues or points – your challenge is to formulate your own such table and probably in a good deal more detail. It also includes, in the final line, some thoughts on outcomes to avoid in each case.

Rules of engagement

Use this exercise as a means of agreeing the *rules of engagement* for each function with each classification of customer. First, agree them internally – I have seen some businesses go as far as having each function agree a number of days that can be committed to each customer classification – a useful approach perhaps in a situation where the functions have not been much involved to date.

Then, and in a process not dissimilar to the creation of service-level agreements with customers, you might choose to come to formal agreements with some customers. It is often with the Maintenance Accounts, where you wish to 'free up your energy', that this can be most valuable.

Step 6. Communication, alignment and implementation

Having expended all this time and effort be sure that the whole organization is now behind the decisions and the implications of the classification process. The extent to which you involved a broad team at Steps 1 through to 5 will have some impact on the ease or otherwise of this concluding step in the process. Persuasion through involvement is a sound principle in this matter.

It may be wise to double-check three key issues:

1. Does each function recognize the need for the classifications, and the basis upon which they have been made?
2. Does each function understand and accept the implications of the customer distinction profiles?
3. Will each function now give full and active support to the plans for each customer type?

Simple enough questions, but having them confirmed will increase everyone's confidence that the operation of a true value machine has come one very important step closer.

Table 5.1 _Customer distinction profiles_

Basis for Distinction	Key Account	Key Development Account	Maintenance Account	Opportunistic Account
Return on investment	• Measured over a minimum 2-3 year period • 'Life Time Value'	• Be prepared to invest up front • Have a clear timetable for anticipated returns • Regular reviews	• Constant attention to enhancing profitability • Take an 'accountants' viewpoint on costs	• Returns must be instant
At what level must we 'understand the customer'?	• Business strategy • Vision and drivers • Market position • View of our competitors • Vendor ratings	• Prepare analysis using the full Diagnostic Toolkit	• Continually monitor for changes in their business strategy that might cause us to reclassify the account	• Current needs
Nature of our contractual commitment	• Full contract designed to promote trust and confidence, as a platform for developing full partnership	• 'Letter of intent' approach, outlining aspirations and expectations • No financial penalties	• Full contract designed to protect current business and build barriers to exit	• No contracts
Relationship and level of contacts	• Diamond Team • Contact matrix • GROWs for all KA Team members	• Focus on the key sponsors and influencers • Involve senior management ASAP	• Seek increasing efficiency of contacts • Make greater use of 'inside sales' team	• Bow-tie relationship
Account plan	• Full written KA plan • Focus on long term growth and profitability	• Draft plan • Focus on short term wins	• Summary plan • Focus on building barriers to exit	• No written plan • Sales forecast
Customer's perception of us	• Their No 1 'helper' • A strategic supplier • Supplier of >60% share	• A bringer of specific and targeted improvements • A key supplier	• Steady and reliable • Eager to keep our business	• Commercially astute • 'We can do a deal with these guys'
Allocation of resource	• Agreed internally on an annual basis • Agreed with customer against clear returns	• Allocated against clear and realistic targets • Timetable of ROI	• Continually withdraw resources where there is no risk of a negative result	• Sales only
Provision of services	• Formally agreed service levels • Formal access to R&D	• Allocated against clear and realistic targets • Timetable of ROI	• Standard Technical Service	• Always charged at commercial rates
Nature and number of projects	• Projects formally agreed by the account team • Financial investment where required	• Small list of highly targeted projects with clear criteria for success	• Provide 'copy/paste' projects	• Only short term projects • No financial support
Availability of technology	• Full collaboration • High speed of delivery	• Top speed of delivery • Tailored 'new' technology	• Limited support on 'modifications' • Medium speed of delivery	• Existing 'off the shelf' technology • No development work
Pricing	• Value based	• Market based	• Value based	• Tactical, based on our available capacity
Overall Strategy	• Farmer • Long term focus	• Focused hunter • Move to farmer ASAP • Short-term wins to establish credibility	• Seeking 'Lock in' • Raising barriers to exit	• Opportunistic hunter
Outcomes to avoid….	• Higher than justified 'cost to serve' • KAM Bureaucracy	• Getting locked into commitments with little or no return	• Becoming complacent • Treating the customer as 2nd class citizen	• Destabilising the market

6

Account management – being appropriate

In Chapter 5 we identified four broad customer classifications – Key Accounts, Key Development Accounts, Maintenance Accounts and Opportunistic Accounts – and through the process of *customer distinction* sketched out some appropriate relationship strategies for each of those classifications. This chapter will explore in a good deal more detail the nature of those relationships, and demonstrate how the task of 'being appropriate' is more than just good sense but contributes significantly to the development of the value machine.

Relationships are important, but not simply because they exist. Building relationships takes time, they can eat up valuable resources without anyone realizing it, and *in themselves* they don't promise any particular return. Plenty of apparently 'good' relationships are merely cosy arrangements with 'friends' – and we all know the panic that sets in when those 'friends' move on…

It is easy to sink into complacency when you *think* you know everyone, and even if you *do* know everyone that in itself doesn't promise better rewards. Indeed, all too often the result of such cosiness and complacency is a customer with the best prices, best terms, best services and the 'life of Riley'.

Let's be clear about what is meant by a 'good relationship'. For some it is a term synonymous with 'being liked'. We're all human, and it's nice to be liked, but it's a poor basis for the kind of returns we seek from our investments. In the world of the value machine there are three elements to a 'good' relationship: being appropriate to the strategic intent behind the relationship, involving the right people from both sides, and building mutual respect through relevant activities.

Chapter 7 will look at the question of the 'right people', as part of the value machine's matching activity, while Chapters 8 and 9 will provide a number of analytical processes by which we might arrive at the 'relevant activities'. This chapter will look at how we find and construct the most appropriate relationship, and method of account management, based on the strategic intent shared between customer and supplier.

But first, one more thought on our cosseted customer living the 'life of Riley' – just how might they regard us? They may seem pleased to see us, there may even be a reasonable chance they will like us, but will they respect us?

Next time you visit your doctor, take a look around their surgery. You will see an impressive array of pharmaceutical company logos, stamped on everything from pens and note pads to mouse mats and even wall clocks. I have often wondered what the NHS bill for stationery would be without this staggering flood of 'gifts'. All these things are supplied by 'friendly' representatives trained in the finer skills of 'interpersonal relationships'. So I asked my own doctor what he made of it all – was it appropriate? 'They've got too much money,' he said, 'and I don't mind relieving them of some of it.' So does he like them? If they don't stay too long, and get to the pens and other 'goodies' quickly, he 'tolerates' them. Does he respect them? I can't print his reply...

THE STRATEGIC INTENT

If we remember (and don't suppose that I am about to let you forget) that our customers are investments, then the question of forming appropriate relationships becomes a great deal easier. Some customers will deserve more attention than others because of their better returns. If returns are reckoned to be low we should aim to have the minimum relationship necessary appropriate to those returns. Indeed, this should be our objective even where the returns are likely to be high – the *minimum* relationship necessary for those returns.

It is all too easy to throw people at a customer, and all too easy to damage our profitability through soaring costs, and damage our prospects with other customers by 'stealing' resources that might have gone to them, perhaps even to irritate our favoured customer by what they see as inappropriate over-attention. Thinking in terms of 'minimums' is a good discipline when managing investments.

Figure 6.1 illustrates a range of possible minimums – four different levels of account management practice – each being appropriate to its circumstances.

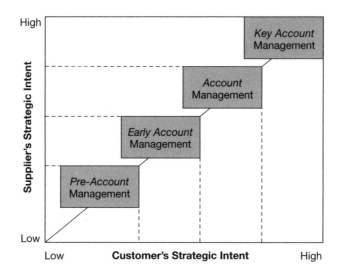

Figure 6.1 *The account management journey*
Adapted from a model first developed by AF Millman and KJ Wilson (1994)

The appropriateness of the relationship is based on the relative 'strategic intents' of both supplier and customer; that is to say, the extent to which each side sees value to be gained from putting effort into the relationship. At the lower end of the spectrum, the intent may involve little more than the ability to place and receive an order, for which the simplest of relationships (if relationship at all) will be required. The higher we go, the greater will be the expectation of value and return and the greater the need and desire for a more committed form of relationship.

The idea of greater 'commitment' might be characterized in two ways. First, an increase in the points of contact (what some refer to as 'touch-points') between supplier and customer, moving from a simple 1:1 relationship through to a more complex team-on-team-based arrangement. Second, the development of the relationship from the short-term transactional basis of 'doing deals' towards one of genuine 'collaboration'; working together with shared objectives and aspirations.

Straight away you will see the need for mutuality of intent, an issue we will return to later. Something else begins to become clear, and a very important realization, that at the higher levels of strategic intent there can be value in the relationship itself, quite apart from the products or services it exists to represent. It will be the relationship that provides the opportunity to learn together, to work on joint developments and to enhance the value proposition to the benefit of both sides.

NAVIGATING THE JOURNEY

The model shown at Figure 6.1 is described as a 'journey' because it is not static: both customers and suppliers change over time and so do their relative strategic intentions. Customers may grow less attractive and we should be eager to reassess the nature of our commitment in such circumstances – the world is too full of complex relationships with customers that are no longer deserving of them.

In navigating the journey we might observe three broad requirements for success: recognizing the need for time, recognizing the need for mutuality, and knowing when to stop.

Management over time

Perhaps we want to advance a customer relationship upwards through these steps or modes of account management. Such things take time. If anyone in a company is guilty of short-termism it is usually senior management. The leadership team has a responsibility to make time available, where it is required. Of course, where a customer is best left at a lower level of commitment then results should be expected much faster. It is ironic that bosses tend to be impatient with the wrong customers and the wrong sales people – a Maintenance Account that doesn't provide instant results is one to be annoyed about, a Key Development Account that doesn't perform straight off requires patience. The art of leadership is in recognizing the different time horizons for each customer – something included in the customer distinction exercise described in Chapter 5 (see Table 5.1).

Moreover, progress along the path does not happen of its own accord. Progress must be sought, consciously, and by both sides, and managed with great care and diplomacy. This is not place for a 'bull in a china shop' account manager, treading on toes (as often within their own organization as within the customer's) as they try to force the customer on.

The need for mutuality

The best relationships are found when both sides share much the same strategic intent, and progress upwards along the path described will demand such mutuality. It is not possible, and certainly not wise, to force a more involved relationship on to a customer without their consent. In this sense, the relationship you get can only be the relationship you deserve.

Again we see the need for patience. It is not unusual for the supplier's strategic intent to be some way ahead of their customer's, and that can lead to frustration, disappointment, and the wrath of management. This can all be avoided if we properly understand the challenges of being appropriate.

Figure 6.2 illustrates the peril of stepping outside the boundaries of mutual progression and slipping into one of two 'frustration zones' – the supplier's, or the customer's.

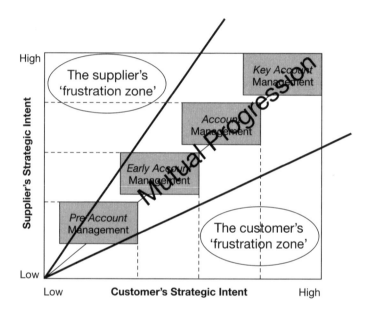

Figure 6.2 *The frustration zones*
Adapted from a model first developed by AF Millman and KJ Wilson (1994)

If the supplier gets too far ahead of the customer, then they are unlikely to secure any of the gains for which they hope. At best, the supplier is frustrated. Worse, the supplier is wasting the customer's time – I have heard a customer say that a supplier was fired because they had 'ideas beyond their station'. The supplier is also wasting their own time, and if this kind of thing is repeated too many times the damage caused can be huge.

If the supplier's intent lags behind the customer's, then they cannot be surprised if that supplier should look elsewhere for someone who will give the time and attention required for the proper fulfilment of their hopes. I have also heard a customer say that a supplier was fired because 'all they had was good products'.

Knowing when to stop...

Remember the idea of 'the minimums'. Taking the relationship beyond the point at which you and the customer are satisfied with the outcomes is unnecessary and potentially damaging. Knowing when to stop is as much a challenge of Account Management as is that of taking a relationship to the very top; perhaps it is a greater one. There is, in any good team, an air of excitement, fuelled by that team's enthusiasm, as relationships move closer to the full Key Account Management stage; putting on the brakes can feel like an anticlimax, perhaps even a failure.

Good leadership will make it plain that things are quite otherwise, and should make sure to reward those behaviours that adhere to the twin principles of _being appropriate_ and striving for the _minimum relationship necessary_.

Take care that those involved in the Account Management journey do not mistake it for a race. This is not about seeing who can take their customer to the end of the path the quickest. If there is any sense of competition at all between account managers, then it is this: who was most _appropriate_, and who managed their case with the _minimum_ resources necessary?

ACCOUNT MANAGEMENT

At whatever stage we position a customer (and note that they go half way to positioning themselves based on their own level of strategic intent towards us) we must practice some form of _Account Management_. The term has increasingly been used to describe relationships with only the more important customers, with the unfortunate result that too little thought is given to the management of the less important customers. As we saw in Chapter 5, our ability to free up energy (see Figure 5.7) by finding new ways of managing our relationships with customers classified 'below the line' in the K.A.I.S.M. is part of the challenge of a true value machine. That a relationship or methodology is simple doesn't stop it being Account Management.

Figure 5.7 also introduced three broad approaches to the relationship management task – _hunting, farming_, and _harvesting_, as they related to the four customer classifications:

1. Opportunistic Account – Hunting;
2. Key Development Account – Hunting;
3. Key Account – Farming;
4. Maintenance Account – Harvesting.

What we are trying to describe are the *lead* attitudes and behaviours required in each case, as a guide, not a rulebook. Customers and their opportunities are too complex to be summed up in three approaches, but a guide is no bad thing.

The Hunter and the Opportunistic Account

This one is simple – the territory of decades of sales practice – spot the opportunities and go for the kill, as fast as possible and with minimum disruption to the activities of colleagues. The hunter hunts for a simple purpose, the kill, and to eat. It is deliberately short-term with no view to future development. Of course if we can arrange to make a similar kill on a regular basis then all the better, but the purpose will remain the same.

The Hunter and the Key Development Account

This starts with the realization that a good deal of progress has to be made with this customer – at present they prefer our competitors. We need to get our foot in various doors, identify the key influencers, and while our eye is certainly on the future we must also make sure of bringing home some short-term successes. If this sounds much like the hunter and the opportunistic account scenario, there are two important differences. First, the purpose is not to eat, but to learn, to impress, to gain access, to ingratiate. Future development is more important than present gain – the short-term successes are intended to build support and momentum, not to fill accountants' stomachs. Second, the sales professionals should be seeking to involve their colleagues from appropriate functions at the earliest opportunity. With Key Development Accounts we should not hunt alone.

It is still common to find that the Account Managers responsible for such customers are picked from the more junior ranks – it being thought the experience will be good for them (or sometimes, and more cynically, that the chances of success are slim). Or else the senior Key Account Managers are given two or three Development Accounts apiece, 'to keep them sharp'. Both ideas mistake the task in hand – perhaps the toughest in the book – to take a customer who is clearly important to our future, but who at present is happier with a competitor, or might not even know who we are, and develop that customer into a long-term partner. En route it may be necessary to develop new and unique value propositions, while all the while ensuring a proper long-term return for the efforts applied. This is no task for an inexperienced sales rep or part-time KA Manager.

The Farmer and the Key Account

The farmer has the happy position of an existing relationship and existing business. Their aim is to maximize the returns from these two advantages, both over the long and the short term. They will have a team of experts at their disposal, and theirs is the job of a Business Manager, adjusting those resources to fit the opportunities, always with an eye on the resultant profitability.

In case the term 'farmer' suggests someone conservative and static, we have in mind here a more dynamic version of the profession, never happy with the status quo, always wanting to improve the business, but ever conscious that economies will be in order should the opportunities start to thin.

The Harvester and the Maintenance Account

These are customers where we are 'in', but they don't represent our most attractive future. Nobody in their right mind would want to lose them on that account, but anyone in a value machine frame of mind would realize that they represent profit today, the task being to harvest the fruits of earlier investments. In the terminology of the Boston Matrix, they are the businesses *cash cows*, and you are welcome to *milk* rather than *harvest* if you prefer.

THE RELATIONSHIP MODELS

Figure 6.3 shows how we might, using the broad approaches already discussed, design four models of customer relationships, one for each step in the Account Management journey. It also indicates a very important line, the point at which the relationship moves from being the solo responsibility of sales, to a team activity. This is not an easy line to cross, in either direction.

The models increase in their level of commitment and involvement as we move upwards in the journey, recognizing the increasingly complex circumstances encountered:

- the complexity of the decision-making process (on both sides);
- the value of those decisions;
- the level of investment;
- the level of interdependency between supplier and customer ('lock-in');
- the level of risk, for both parties (the stakes being higher);
- the effective management of risk (through collaborative processes);
- the value to the customer of the supplier's proposition;

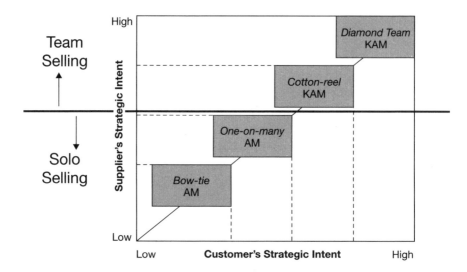

Figure 6.3 *The relationship models*

- the supplier's competitive advantage;
- the supplier reward.

A note on the figures

Figures 6.4 through to 6.10 use as their example a typical B2B manufacturing circumstance. This is of course only an example, and the functions and job titles used are not intended as any form of template or instruction. Nor do the numbers of contacts between supplier and customer suggest any ideal state – you must of course determine what is right for you in your own circumstance.

In between the four models lie many further options and variations on the theme. Treat them as indicators of what things might look like at different stages of the journey – we are charting various courses and it is always helpful to know what the scenery might look like as we pass it by.

The 'Bow-tie' relationship

Figure 6.4 illustrates perhaps the most common supplier/customer relationship of them all – the Bow-tie.

- The principal contact is between two people – usually the salesperson and the buyer.
- The relationship may be competitive – each seeking to gain advantage – it may sometimes even be confrontational.

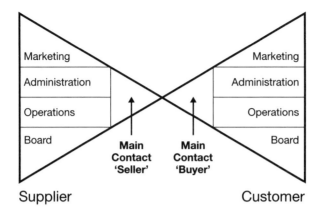

Figure 6.4 _Bow-tie account management_
Adapted from McDonald, Millman and Rogers (1996)

- The buyer may see any attempt to gain access to other contacts as a threat to their own position and power.
- The seller may regard any attempted involvement by others from their own company as unwelcome interference.
- Both seller and buyer regard the relationship as one that gives them a high degree of 'control'.
- Price discussions probably dominate.
- The supplier focuses on increased volume.
- The sales professional is trained in transactional skills such as negotiation.
- The focus is on short-term and transactional dealings.
- Buyers may use performance criteria that are not shared with the supplier.
- The customer is still assessing alternative suppliers.
- Disputes can lead to long-term breaks in supply.

This is the archetypal hunter–killer model, in its solo guise. It has plenty of things going for it; it is fast, it is to the point, its objectives are clear, the seller feels in control, and it uses the absolute minimum resource (other than selling through remote means – tele-sales, internet portals, etc).

So, for a customer where the mutual intentions are basic – placing and receiving orders – it is ideal, keeping costs to a minimum on both sides. It is also attractive where there may be fears regarding the customer's true intentions – a good 'arm's length' approach. It is also where almost any new relationship is likely to start.

There is a particular danger inherent in this model – resulting from the high level of control experienced by the seller and buyer – the danger of just staying there. Why move on when everything is comfortable and the orders are coming in?

Well, for a customer higher up the path of strategic intent, the following lists just some of the serious weaknesses in this model (surely enough incentive to move on if the opportunity justifies?):

- Poor knowledge of the customer's true needs.
- Poor knowledge of the customer's decision-making process.
- Plays into the hands of a restrictive buyer.
- Does the supplier know its true value?
- Expertise on both sides is seriously underutilized – the seller and the buyer are expected to be all-round experts – an unlikely scenario.
- Messages from other functions are mistranslated (and littered with 'Chinese whispers').
- Projects and activities are held up by the sales/purchasing bottleneck.
- Low security of tenure due to the over-reliance on one relationship.
- Sales people can become 'kingpins' who cannot be promoted for fear of losing the business – a sad end to a promising career…

The 'One-on-many' relationship

Figure 6.5 illustrates what many would consider as 'advanced selling'; some might even dignify it by the title of 'strategic selling'. This is where the sales professional breaks out of the restrictions imposed by the 1:1 Bow-tie, and establishes direct contact with a range of other people in the customer.

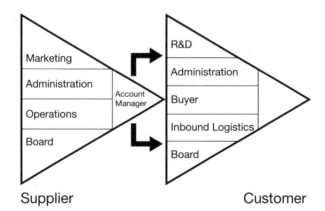

Figure 6.5 *One-on-many account management*

The seller broadens their base of contacts – this may be a reconnaissance, looking for further opportunities, or a desire for a less transactional relationship.

- If this results from the buyer's encouragement, then this is probably indicative of an increase in the customer's strategic intent – a recognition of the supplier's need to understand more about the true circumstances and needs, or to manage interactions with a broader range of functions.
- If this is sought without the buyer's encouragement, then take extreme care – buyers can be sensitive to such ventures. If it is without their permission, then don't do it – buyers have a way of getting you back for such cheek...
- The seller continues to work alone, either through lack of resources in their own business, or through a deliberate desire to minimize investment costs until a better understanding of the opportunity is gained, or perhaps simply to maintain control.

Price will probably still dominate discussions, but the buyer will perhaps be more open to discussions around 'cost-in-use', based on the seller's greater knowledge.

- Sellers may start to be aware of performance criteria beyond the purchasing department.
- The seller may be able to develop aspects of 'lock-in', beyond the buyer, but by restricting the buyer's subsequent freedom to look elsewhere this might in turn lead to the buyer's reluctance to allow such contacts – take care...

Disputes can sometimes be moderated by people beyond the seller/buyer interface.

Perhaps we might think of this model as that of the *clever* hunter. If the intention is a kind of reconnaissance – to better understand our value, or to see where new opportunities may lie – and if the intention is to involve others if those opportunities justify (ie moving on to the *cotton-reel* model – see Figure 6.6), and the nature of the value requires it, then this can be a thoroughly effective advance on the Bow-tie.

If the reconnaissance proves fruitless, then the best move may be to slip back to the bow-tie relationship – sustaining such *one-on-many* relationships for any period of time can be hugely draining on the sales professional's time and energy. Aim to make this a staging post, not the endgame.

The 'Cotton-reel' relationship

Figure 6.6 illustrates the point at which the sales professional steps over the line from solo account manager to a team-based 'Key' Account Manager, albeit with the smallest of teams at this stage – a duet. It is at this point that the sales professional makes two further transitions: from 'seller' to 'business manager', and from 'hunter' to 'farmer'.

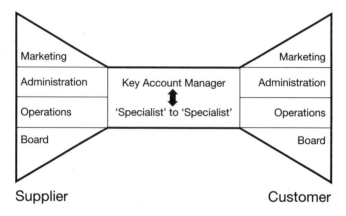

Figure 6.6 *Cotton-reel key account management*

- Direct contacts between supplier and customer functions are established, through the auspices of the Account Manager, pairing 'specialists' or 'experts'.
- The purpose may be to facilitate greater mutual understanding, to develop new opportunities, or to build joint-managed projects.
- There is a significant increase in time required to brief and coach.
- An increase in internal communications (it is to be hoped!) – with a potential burden of excess information or bureaucracy if this is not managed appropriately.
- An improvement in customer awareness and customer focus within the supplier's organization.
- Knowledge begins to translate into action.
- Increasing opportunities for 'lock-in' through genuinely customer-focused value propositions that might speak more about value than price or cost.
- Increased trust and openness developing with the customer – disputes become things to be resolved through the involvement of the appropriate people.

There is no question that this stage is hard work, for all involved. Introducing colleagues to customers takes time (that is if you wish to avoid numerous subsequent problems), and it is unlikely that returns on this effort are immediate. This stage is the start of true long-term investment in the customer.

New skills and behaviours will be required by all involved. The Account Manager will need to become a top-class coach, while the non-sales people will need to develop their technique in front of the customer. Easily enough said, but in fact these can be two huge challenges, and quite enough to put both parties off the idea. If such advances are to be made then the leadership team will need to encourage, coach and provide training where required.

The leadership team must also ensure that those involved have sufficient time for this relationship, in two senses. First, time in the most obvious sense of days in the week – don't expect Account Managers to be able to handle too many of these types of relationship at once, and don't expect their colleagues to be suddenly available for dozens of customers. Second, time in the sense of when results are expected. This model will be typical of the relationship with a Key Development Account and our customer distinction strategy (see Chapter 5) should have taken good note of the time horizons and the expected return on investments.

Parallel cotton-reels

In some cases these duets may occur between more than just one colleague and the customer, resembling the picture illustrated at figure 6.7 – a series of parallel Cotton-reels.

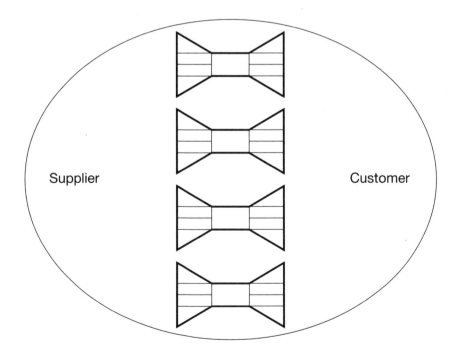

Figure 6.7 _Parallel cotton-reels_

This is of course a Diamond Team in the making (see Figure 6.8). We might ask then, what is the difference between a Diamond Team and a set of parallel Cotton-reels? Is a Diamond Team just a fat Cotton-reel?

I have heard it argued that Cotton-reels might be transitory, while Diamond Teams are permanent. Often true, at least in relative terms, but I wouldn't want to make it a rule – for one thing, given the necessary rate of change with all customer relationships, diamonds are most certainly *not* forever…

A better distinction is to say that a Diamond Team is just that, *a team*, working in concert, whereas the parallel cotton-reels may be isolated from each other. This is of course precisely one of the dangers of this stage, and the KA Manager must resolve either to proceed towards the control and discipline of a genuine team, or live with the workload (and the frequent frustrations) of juggling so many balls at one time.

A Key Account Manager was struggling to make this stage work. Their biggest frustration was the limitation that each of the newly introduced people put on themselves. Each one showed great reluctance to be involved any further than achieving their own narrow objectives, which were often less than the KA Manager hoped from them. They were certainly not in any sense part of a team with bigger ambitions.

During a coaching session with one of these people, on being asked why they had such reluctance, it became clear that fear lay at the bottom of things. 'When I visit the customer,' they said, 'I get in and out as quickly as possible.' 'Why is that?' asked the KA Manager. 'Well,' came the reply, 'what if I was to meet someone important, and they asked me something difficult?'

Easy to laugh, or to be cynical about the customer-facing capabilities of non-sales professionals, but if you are to make this stage work, or wish to build beyond it, then such fears must be thoroughly overcome.

The 'Diamond Team' relationship

Figure 6.8 illustrates the next step beyond parallel Cotton-reels, where the individuals on the supplier side have formed a genuine team, working in concert with their opposite numbers who, ideally, though not always, also see themselves as a team. Remember, the Figure is just an example and there is no requirement for you to mimic the functions involved or the numbers involved – Diamond Teams can comprise as few as three people, or they might run to dozens (though only if appropriate of course!).

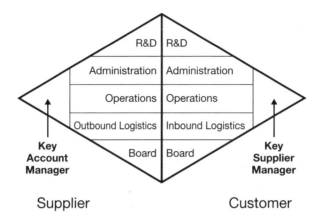

Figure 6.8 *Diamond Team key account management*
Adapted from McDonald, Millman and Rogers (1996)

- The individuals involved are aware of their role within a team, and operate accordingly.
- Each member has clarity on their own goals, roles and obligations to the team.
- Contacts are secured at all levels, from operational to senior management.
- The KA Manager's role is principally one of coordination – they may even choose to step aside from the day-to-day sales activities, delegating those instead to a sales professional within the Diamond Team.
- It is very likely that Key Supplier Status is awarded – few customers will allow such involvement by suppliers with any other than key suppliers.
- The customer mirrors the KA Manager with a Key Supplier Manager whose focus is on developing the supplier's capabilities rather than challenging them.
- Relationships are based on trust – they have to be for such a relationship to function. The supplier's security of tenure is high – though they must take care not to become complacent.
- Access to people is facilitated and information is shared – perhaps through shared communication networks (viz. intranets).
- Supplier and customer staff may be trained together, focusing on collaborative teamwork rather than transactional skills (viz. negotiation).
- Shared business plans may be developed.
- The customer gets the supplier's new ideas first – they may also have an expectation for some measure of exclusivity.
- Continuous improvement is expected from those suppliers.
- Clear 'vendor ratings' and 'performance measures' are discussed and agreed.

- 'Value' is the watchword, sought through integrated business processes (value inside), and/or through a focus on the customer's markets (value beyond).
- Collaboration speeds the pace of joint activities – New Product Development can be hugely enhanced through such teams.
- Longer term contracts are likely to be more common, including agreements on pricing, which is usually more stable and less transactional – it may even be that the higher levels of trust in this relationship allow for transparency of costs and margins, from both sides.
- 'Step-outs' are permitted – that is to say, disagreements are allowed – the supplier must not always say yes for the relationship to continue.

This is a long list, and taken as a whole such a description would be wildly optimistic; if all of these characteristics were to exist at once then you would have found the Holy Grail of KAM indeed! Regard them as a list of potential ambitions, or as a checklist against which you can judge to what extent you are still travelling towards a Diamond Team KAM relationship, or have arrived.

This is of course the relationship most likely to bring the most benefit to the value machine, through its enhanced knowledge and collaborative working practices, but it is also the model with the most implications; implications on capabilities, on time, on resources and on money. Diamond Teams represent significant investments of all these things.

There are, inevitably, some dangers with such teams, and a few 'health warnings' might be timely.

Curbing misplaced enthusiasm...

The collaboration inherent in such teams speeds the pace of joint activities, but be warned, as things move more quickly, so the risk of saying or doing the wrong things also increases. We saw how the KA Manager had to take on the role of coach to facilitate the new contacts developed at the Cotton-reel stage, well, at the Diamond Team stage they must not only enhance those skills, to become a 'super-coach', but also take on the additional role of 'super-coordinator'.

That highly enthusiastic IT expert that you have brought in might take you down some unwanted paths if left to their own devices, as might that young and confident R&D chemist, *as might the boss...*

The CEO of a multinational manufacturer was visiting one of their business unit's distributors – a Key Account. The business unit sold high-spec plastic/glass panels, used, among other things, to build all-round-viewing squash courts. The distributor suggested that having such a squash court on their premises would be a great sales aid, much better than the sales brochures. The CEO readily agreed – a free 'sample' would be installed. It was certainly an aid, but unfortunately the CEO had not been aware of two facts.

First, he didn't know that the cost ran into tens of thousands of pounds. Second, and in a sense worse, he didn't know that the distributor had been asking that selfsame question for some time, and had been given the selfsame answer by the KA Manager: 'Sure, when you pay your bills on time, and stock our new ranges, and employ two new sales reps, and meet the following targets...'

So, whose fault was it that a 'free squash court' was given away with nothing gained in return? The CEO should have known better, but the KA Manager is equally, if not more, responsible. They should have briefed the CEO. KA Managers are responsible for all communications, transactions and activities between supplier and customer.

The management/authority dilemma

Few, if any, of the members of a Diamond Team will work directly for the KA Manager. There is no formal management relationship. Some members may be senior to the KA Manager. All (if they are worth their membership) are 'smarter' than the KA Manager, with regard to their own speciality.

In such circumstances it is easy for things to run out of control. Figure 6.9 illustrates one outcome of such lack of control, and certainly the relationship to be most avoided.

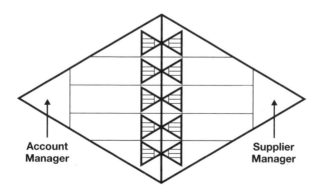

Figure 6.9 *The relationship to avoid*

There are multiple contacts with the customer, but each one acts as its own Bow-tie, independent of the others, and with no overall control from the KA Manager. It may even be that the KA Manager has no knowledge of some of these contacts. This is not a team; this is anarchy. The customer may be frustrated by this – demanding one point of contact in place of the chaos, or worse; they might just take advantage of it – picking off the weakest links, one by one...

Building a genuine team from diverse resources, and without line management responsibility is a tough task that calls for high levels of skill (and diplomacy) from the KA Manager, but it also calls for a high level of support from the leadership team. From time to time non-collaborative heads may need knocking together. From time to time the KA Manager's authority may not run far enough. At such times the support of the leadership team is vital – not to take over, not to become the KA Manager, but to provide support. Sad to say, not all leadership teams are up to this suppression of their egos.

No opposite number?

What if there is no mirror image to the KA Manager in the Diamond team, no Key Supplier Manager? They don't always exist, and their absence will certainly slow down progress towards a truly integrated team-on-team relationship. I know of at least one KA Manager who, aware of this problem, worked hard to build his main contact up into this position. The contact didn't have a formal job title to that effect, but they did start to perform the role desired – providing greater access, facilitating the team-on-team relationship, and helping to build the supplier's capabilities rather than simply challenging them.

Bureaucracy, bureaucracy, and bureaucracy...

Diamond Teams can be large, and their management can be daunting. The task of maintaining communications across such diverse groups can become a nightmare. Internal meetings can become so frequent that nobody has time to see the customer any more... Perhaps I exaggerate, but the warning should be clear. The answer is simply not to allow things to develop in that way.

Take meetings for instance. Does the whole Diamond Team have to gather for every meeting? Try to identify what we might call a 'core' team, perhaps of three or four people, perhaps those with the most significant customer contacts and roles. Such a team can meet more easily, and as required. The wider team – let's call them the 'surround team' (some say the 'supporting' team, but I don't like the idea of hierarchy and subservience implied) – may meet far less frequently, as a whole group perhaps only once a year, and in some cases not even that.

Recognize the true costs

Diamond Teams don't come for free – but so often the real costs are not considered, or accounted for. People's time costs money, and the KA Manager is spending that money by bringing people into their team. And don't expect to establish a Diamond Team while cutting travel budgets – these relationships require personal contact, particularly in the early days.

Does the KA Manager not have a customer-facing role?

In extreme cases, they may not, but for 99 per cent of the cases of course they will – so why does the model (Figure 6.8) suggest otherwise?

The model is drawn to stress the extreme difference in the task between that of the sales professional in a Bow-tie relationship and the KA Manager in a Diamond Team. In the former, they have to be a great salesperson. In the latter, they have to be a great business manager. In so doing it does appear to exclude the KA Manager from customer contact, and that is perhaps a deficiency. Perhaps the picture shown in Figure 6.10 might serve the purpose better?

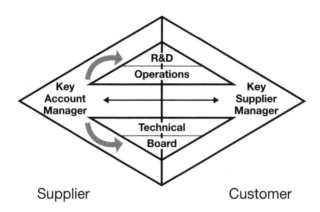

Figure 6.10   _The KA Manager's customer contact_

So why not show it this way in the first place? The main reason is the need to avoid any assumption on the KA Manager's part that once they have put their colleagues in touch with their opposite numbers they can go back to their old job of looking after the buyer.

Yet even Figure 6.9 doesn't represent the full truth, which will surely have the KA Manager involved with a number of those on the customer's side. The Diamond Team is a concept, and the model is only that, a model. For a specific 'map' of the relationship we need to turn to the contact matrix, of which more will be said in Chapter 7.

Just too many...

It will be clear that true Diamond Teams are a rarity, and for all sorts of reasons. One of these reasons at least is within our own control – we should not aim to have too many. They are complex, and need careful management – too many and they drift out of control. They are significant investments deserving significant returns – too many and we dilute our efforts. To repeat an earlier assertion – better to be great just a few times, than mediocre on plenty of occasions...

Trust and partnership – real world, or myth?

High levels of trust are required in a Diamond Team; trust between the members of the supplier team, and trust between supplier and customer. Trust develops over time, through good practice, through the keeping of promises, through the kind of respect that comes from being appropriate, and from being open. You must decide how far you can go with being 'open' – what is regarded as commendable honesty in one business environment might well be seen as sheer stupidity in another.

A supplier has found a solution to one of their Key Account's manufacturing problems. This wasn't the cause for celebration that you might imagine because the solution didn't need the supplier's help, rather, it involved a tweak to the customer's own manufacturing process that would allow them to use a cheaper competitor material.

So what does the supplier do: tell the customer or withhold the solution? The former is certainly collaborative, but is it foolhardy? The latter leaves open the awful prospect of being found out: 'so you knew but you didn't tell us'. I leave you to decide (but here's a clue – they are a Key Account...).

The value machine seeks true partnerships with a handful of customers, the genuine Key Accounts, and yet we must always be careful with this word, 'partnership'. Wait to hear it on the customer's lips first. Even then, take care. Perhaps your customer will use the lure of 'partnership' as a trap: 'Let's work in partnership', they say, meaning: 'You give us your cost breakdowns, and then we'll take you to the cleaners...'.

> A pig and a chicken decide to go into partnership together – it was the chicken's idea. They decide to go into the catering business, specializing in traditional English breakfasts, and because it was the chicken's idea it presents its ideas first.
>
> 'It's a great idea this partnership thing,' it clucks, 'and I tell you what, why don't I supply the eggs, and you supply the bacon...'.

At the start of this chapter I suggested there were three elements required to justify the label 'good relationship': being appropriate to the strategic intent behind the relationship, involving the right people from both sides, and building mutual respect through relevant activities. This chapter has focused mainly on the first of the three, though if this is achieved it goes a long way to achieving the respect desired in the third. For the second element – involving the right people from both sides – we have suggested some models by which we manage the involvement of people beyond the seller/buyer interface, but we have yet to identify precisely who those people might be. We have the box but not the contents.

In the next chapter we will turn to the twin questions: 'who must we know in the customer?' and 'who must we involve from our own organization?'. It is with these questions that we begin the matching process and so start to breath real life into the workings of the value machine.

Part III

Matching

7

The people

In Chapter 3 we began an examination of the fuel that powers the value machine, identifying two key ingredients: the raw data about our own business and the raw data about our customers. In this chapter we will examine a third ingredient of that fuel, and perhaps the most important of all – the people.

It is the people that truly breathe life into the value machine, rather as fire breathes life into a steam engine. Without fire the steam engine is an interesting enough thing, but only so much cold metal when all is said and done. Add the key ingredient and it becomes a living thing – ask any steam enthusiast! The value machine is much the same.

People may breathe life into the value machine, but they can also clog its pipes – we need to be sure of involving the *right* people. This chapter will consider two key questions: who must we get to know in the customer, and who must we involve from our own side in order to build the kind of collaborative relationships essential to the creation of true value propositions?

We are at the start of the value machine's matching process, bringing together the right people in order to identify the needs, to develop the enhanced value propositions, and to engineer the appropriate rewards – activities and processes to be discussed in Chapters 8 and 9.

THE PROBLEM WITH BUYERS...

We begin with a problem: buyers. In some cases these people exist simply to deny suppliers access to the truth – knowledge of their own value. In other cases they are the supplier's expert guide, opening doors and oiling the wheels of collaboration. The problem is not so much their existence, but knowing with which kind we are dealing.

Where we are considering the making of matches with those customers identified as 'Key Accounts', it is to be hoped that we are dealing with the second category – the enablers – on the basis that for us to have considered a customer as 'Key' we will also be regarded as a significant supplier – the mutuality of strategic intent described in Chapter 6.

But if we are dealing with Key Development Accounts, this mutuality is probably off in the hoped-for future, and we may be in the hands of the first category of buyer, the gatekeeper and blocker, sometimes referred to as 'the abominable no-man'.

Of course, in either scenario, the buyer may only be the front man, 'held hostage' by a variety of people in their own organization, each with a different set of interests and influences. Perhaps the manufacturing department has laid down clear rules on what materials they need, and whom they should come from, and the buyer's teasing promises that they might consider a change of supplier are little more than warm air. In such cases the buyer may be no more than the puppet of those other interests, a rubber stamp, but how many would admit to such a position? This has ever been the supplier's dilemma; is the buyer the real focus of power, or should that be sought else-where, and if so, how, without antagonizing the buyer?

Or they may truly be the 'kingpin' that they say they are; not only there to negotiate the price, but also, and far more importantly, to facilitate a collabo-rative partnership. In such a case we have no need to pursue routes around the buyer... or does that leave us too much in their hands? Another kind of dilemma...

Problems, doubts and dilemmas usually result from a lack of knowledge, or perhaps from misunderstandings over time. History can often be a burden as much as it is a source of learning. In this chapter we look to break free of these problems, doubts and dilemmas through the use of a series of analytical tools, each designed to help us understand the customer's decision-making processes. We have to identify the key players in that most mysterious of entities – the customer's DMU (decision-making unit). This will in turn enable us to plan the most appropriate contact strategy, through two action tools, 'matchmaking' the relationship with our own team of people.

THE CUSTOMER'S DMU

In businesses of any size, despite the assertions of buyers, most important decisions regarding suppliers, or at least the significant suppliers (see Chapter 8 for more on this distinction), are made by groups of people – decision-making units. In some companies, these may be quite formal – project teams, sourcing teams or the procurement committee. In others, they may be so informal as to be unidentifiable; but they are there all the same, working by inference, by nods of the head and the raising of eyebrows.

There are three broad types:

1. authoritarian DMUs;
2. consensus DMUs;
3. consultative DMUs.

The authoritarian DMU

A single person – perhaps the boss, perhaps the owner of a smaller business – will take the decision and impose it on their colleagues and staff, sometimes even against the better judgement of the latter.

For the supplier this is the easiest DMU to influence. If you can identify that individual, gain access to them, and form a proposition that meets their personal needs, the sale is made. But we are looking for more than simply the sale, we are looking for a collaborative partnership, and that will almost certainly necessitate the building of relations with others beyond 'the boss'. This calls for a particular kind of patience, establishing contacts with people who contribute little to the short-term objectives of selling, and where those contacts might even be sources of irritation for the authoritarian decision maker.

The consensus DMU

This involves some kind of 'democracy'. Perhaps all members of the DMU must agree, or maybe it is a case of a majority vote. Typically, consensus DMUs might be found in cooperatives, institutions, the government and civil service, and voluntary groups.

For the supplier this is much harder work, as they must ensure that they meet and persuade at least a majority of members, if not all.

Such decisions are often taken in private, with no supplier access to the 'committee'. The problem here is that you don't always know the mechanism and criteria for their decision. You may win the order, but if you don't know why, maintaining or developing that business might be difficult, and building a collaborative partnership harder still. This calls for a dose of detective work; how does the 'committee' work; who takes note of whom; is it personalities or business criteria that matter?

The consultative DMU

Here there is an appointed decision maker – very often the commercial buyer – who will make the decision based on the views of the key influencers in the DMU. They will consult with those people and decide accordingly.

It is probably the most common of the DMU types, particularly in larger organizations, yet so often it is the toughest one for the supplier to crack – they need to know so much. First – and this is the easy one – who is the appointed decision maker? Next, with whom do they consult? Still further, do they give more weight to one opinion over another? And last – but by no means least – are there any opinions that they positively discount? This calls for an attention to detail, and a nose for the politics of organizations.

THE TOOLKIT

The analysis of the customer DMU is made for two reasons: to understand, and then to act. Figure 7.1 shows a range of tools designed for these two purposes.

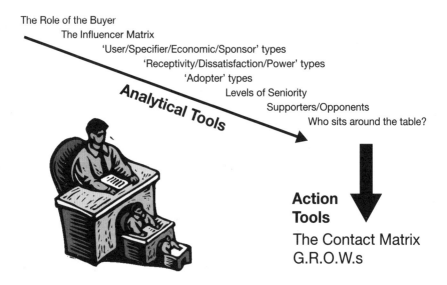

Figure 7.1 *The DMU toolkit*

The 'analytical' tools are not intended for use on every occasion, they represent a toolkit that can be dipped into as suits the circumstance. The 'action' tools should be regarded rather differently: they provide the prime means of managing the matching process with the customer and their importance is such as to make their use almost mandatory.

THE ANALYTICAL TOOLS

The role of the buyer

We should begin by understanding the role of the buyer, the most likely first contact for most suppliers, or if not, the person who comes in later to spoil the party. In Chapter 8 we will look at how they _position_ us as a supplier, and how that determines their strategy towards us, and how we might respond, but for now we will limit our analysis to their role and behaviour as part of the DMU.

Figure 7.2 shows four potential roles or behaviours, based on the level of interest that they show in our activities and propositions, and their level of involvement in the decision-making process.

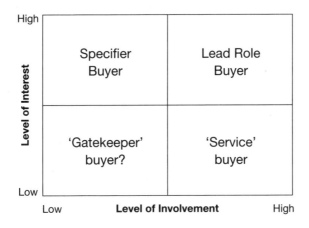

Figure 7.2   _The role of the buyer_

The 'lead' buyer

With both high interest and involvement expect this buyer to take a leading role. It is very likely that the decision under question will have a direct impact on their own measures of performance, which means that the supplier is about to be champion, or sinner. Such buyers may take a positive role in introducing

93

you to others in their organization where those people can contribute to a positive outcome – a true ally if you are considered a worthy supplier. Work closely with such a buyer.

The 'specifier' buyer

A buyer in this position suggests that the real decision is to be made elsewhere but they have been called in for their professional expertise, perhaps helping to set guidelines for others to work by. If closer collaboration is required it is unlikely that this buyer will want to be involved, but they will certainly want to know what is happening. Don't attempt to go around them; rather, seek this buyer's advice on how to proceed, and volunteer the involvement of your own colleagues. Aim to help this buyer meet their obligations.

The 'service' buyer

We might call this the 'reluctant' buyer – performing their role on behalf of someone else, but seeing no real benefit or advantage to themselves. This can be hard going for the supplier, faced with a buyer who doesn't really care. The wise supplier might find ways of volunteering their services to take on some of the buyer's role, but will also take care to demonstrate their ability to be trusted with such involvement. It is important to get beyond this buyer.

The 'gatekeeper' buyer

Why should a buyer who has no interest in your proposition, and no involvement in the decision, still refuse you access to others? Surely they should be pleased to let you get on about your business with others? Such a buyer, contrary to sales folklore, may actually be doing a good job, protecting their organization from the 'interference' of overzealous suppliers.

It may be possible to increase the buyer's interest, through propositions that are relevant to their own objectives. Failing that, the supplier has to get past such a gatekeeper, but only with the gatekeeper's permission – this is vital. Tact and diplomacy is key here, and a good deal of patience. A possible approach might be to suggest that there are others in the supplier's organization better placed to deal with the buyer's colleagues; in other words, it isn't the salesperson trying to bypass the buyer.

The influencer matrix

Figure 7.3 shows the members of the customer's DMU, indicating the level of influence that they have on each other.

		IS INFLUENCED BY...						
		John Smith	Sue Rogers	Terry Paine	Alex Holland	Steph Higgins	Barry Munroe	Alice Hill
THIS PERSON...	John Smith		★★		★★			
	Sue Rogers					★★★		★
	Terry Paine							
	Alex Holland		★★	★				
	Steph Higgins		★					
	Barry Munroe	★★★★★	★★	★★				
	Alice Hill		★★					

Figure 7.3 *The influencer matrix*

If we recall the many challenges presented by a consultative DMU from earlier in the chapter – who is the appointed decision maker, with whom do they consult, do they give more weight to one opinion over another, and are there any opinions that they positively discount? – it will be readily seen how this tool can help.

A start may be made to such a matrix by considering the simple realities of hierarchy and seniority, but beyond that we must recognize the role of personal chemistry, ambition, inter-departmental rivalries, and politics.

The aim is to seek what we might call 'positive influence pathways', or more simply, the best route to particular targets. In the example shown in Figure 7.3 it is clear that John Smith makes a big impression on Barry Monroe, and if Barry Monroe is your ultimate target, then spending time with John Smith could be a sound investment.

Of course, people who wield significant influence, as John Smith does, tend to attract attention, and chances are that plenty of time is already spent with this individual, but what about Sue Rogers? She doesn't pack such a punch with any one individual, but she appears to carry some weight with a broad range of people. Is it worth spending more time with the likes of Sue Rogers?

Completing the matrix...

The knowledge to complete this matrix comes over time, from any and all of those who have contact with the customer (we are of course dealing here with the kind of *customer data* discussed in Chapter 2). In a sense, it is formalizing the kind of gossip that goes on about customers all the time, and gossip is fine, if directed to a positive end. Of course, much of it is hugely subjective, but if it represents the pooled views and observations of the supplier team, and not the solo view of the Account Manager, then it has its own value regardless of that subjectivity: it is a vehicle for stimulating debate and even argument. Arguments can also be fine, provided they too are directed to a positive end – a better understanding of the customer.

User/Specifier/Economic/Sponsor

This tool comes from the excellent work of R B Miller and S E Heiman. Most decision-making units can be seen to contain each of the four 'types of involvement' illustrated in Figure 7.4.

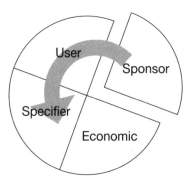

Figure 7.4 *Types of involvement*

An individual's involvement in a particular decision may be limited to just one of these types, or they might have multiple reasons for their involvement. The benefits of understanding these types are significant for any supplier seeking to navigate a path through a complex DMU:

- Focusing on the nature of someone's involvement in the decision can bring far greater clarity than focusing on job titles.
- It helps identify an order of contact: who first, and who last? The arrow in figure 7.4 suggests the most advantageous order, the moral being: know your value before speaking to the people most concerned with money.
- Looking ahead to the matching of contacts, it helps determine who from the supplier team might be best placed to work alongside each individual in the customer's DMU.

The Sponsor

The 'Sponsor' (often referred to as the 'Coach') is someone who wishes you to succeed, for whatever reason, and will help you in your task through the provision of information, advice and support. They may be junior or senior, and they might not even be one of the active decision makers – they just wish you well!

A Sponsor can ease your path through the complexity of the customer's organization, perhaps pointing out to you the specifiers, the users and those with the economic interest. Take their advice.

The User

The User is someone who makes use of the product or service (yours or the competitor's), either actively by physical use, or by receipt of its benefits. They probably have strong views on what they want, based on the problems they encounter, and herein lies their importance – they are the route to true value.

The problem for the supplier is that they are not always the easiest people to contact, especially if a gate-keeping buyer stands in the way. Very often the path to their door is best trodden by people other than sales professionals, and this is where to make full use of the supplier team, whether technical service engineers, customer service staff, merchandisers, or anyone else who has good reason to make contact.

The Specifier

The Specifier is the person who lays down the target outcomes, and any other criteria for the decision. These criteria are the 'brass-tacks' of the decision, and vital to know, but very often they might be set by someone who is at least one step removed from the physical use, and so the reality of the need. We have all been frustrated by such 'theoretical' influencers, people determined to have it their way even though the rest of the organization is crying out for something quite different. Aim to meet with such people once you have met with the users, that way you can help them set better criteria.

The Economic

And so we come to the money interest, the person most interested in, or most influenced by, the financial issues. They are often seen as the most important person in the DMU, perhaps because they will so often be the blocker, and for the most obvious reasons; too expensive, no budget, cheaper alternatives... Unless your aim is to establish whether a budget is available, or perhaps you are a hunter seeking a quick yes/no response, it is usually wise to leave these folk to the end of the selling process. Aim to know your true value before getting in front of someone who says you are too expensive.

Using the analysis

Assuming we have quality data, the uses are many: planning an order of approach, considering the matchmaking of people, preparing cases for each type, identifying the potential sticking points or blocks, but perhaps most importantly of all, identifying your true value, and enhancing it as necessary, before getting locked in to the economic interest.

It is in fact the journey through these contacts that can kick-start the process of value creation: identifying new needs from the users, drawing up new criteria with the specifiers, agreeing the value with the 'economic buyer', and being guided throughout by the sponsor.

Receptivity, dissatisfaction, or power... ?

Figure 7.5 suggests another slicing of the DMU, this time by the existing attitudes, or stances, of those involved.

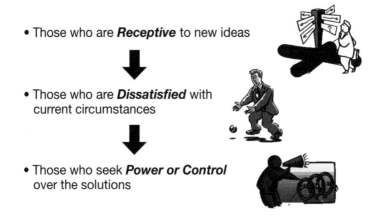

- Those who are **Receptive** to new ideas

- Those who are **Dissatisfied** with current circumstances

- Those who seek **Power or Control** over the solutions

Figure 7.5 *Types of attitude*

In any DMU there will be people likely to be receptive to your ideas (it is to be hoped), people who are dissatisfied with the current situation (it is to be hoped yet more), and people who wish to have power, or control, over the decision (and that one is for sure).

There is a danger that we spend too much time with those who are receptive – we are only human.

There is another danger of being drawn too quickly towards people who demonstrate power – they seem important.

But isn't the key to value creation to be found among the people with the dissatisfaction? A value proposition is usually based on a solution, and a solution needs a problem...

Of course, each attitude type will play its role, in the hands of a supplier focused on the value machine principle. The 'receptive' folk will lead us to the people with the dissatisfaction. The 'dissatisfied' folk will indicate the problems and provide the working partnership for the creation of solutions. The 'power' folk will provide the authority to make things happen – to create the budgets, to form the working parties, and to authorize the supplier collaborations.

Adopter types

People take up new ideas at different rates. Some people like anything new; we might call them 'innovators'. Others might be last in line for change; we might call them 'laggards'. Figure 7.6 illustrates the spectrum of attitudes between these two extremes.

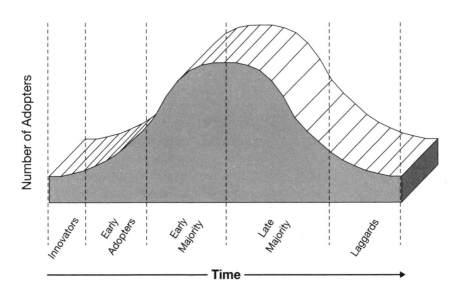

Figure 7.6   _The adopters curve_

This is a model much used by marketing folk as a means of segmenting markets (you might like to add it to the other methods discussed in Chapter 4), targeting effort and tailoring messages. It is equally applicable for the purpose of targeting effort across different members of a DMU, and tailoring the messages in each case.

At the left-hand end of the spectrum, the Innovators and Early Adopters are relatively easy to sell to. They like novelty and the words 'leading-edge', 'risk', 'trial' and 'you're the first' are music to their ears.

At the right-hand end, the Late Majority and the Laggards are much harder. They want evidence and proof. They want to see a track record of success and to know that somebody else has ironed out all the problems.

In the centre, the Early Majority represent the people who come knocking on your door in floods once the idea or product is fairly well established.

Navigating the right path…

Who would start their persuasion task with the Laggards? They do have one benefit to the supplier – they will give them an exhaustive list of the obstacles to come and the hurdles to be jumped. As an exercise in market research, speaking to Laggards has its place.

How about the Innovators? Easy to sell to, certain to say yes… but won't they be just the same when your competitor comes knocking? The real problem with Innovators is what everyone else in the spectrum thinks about them: 'Nutters, crazies, weirdoes, suckers for anything new, and geeks'. Not the best platform on which to base your approach to the next in line. Sell to Innovators by all means, but don't expect them to be the most persuasive influence within their own DMU.

So, once again we see a tool that helps us determine the right order of approach. Its indications might confirm those of other tools, or they might shed new light – either outcome is valuable in what must always be an ongoing debate across the supplier team.

Perhaps its most valuable contribution is in indicating *how* the approach should be made. Each adopter type requires its own approach, its own language, and the right selection of contact from the supplier team. People are usually best persuaded by people like themselves – don't send one of your own Laggards to stimulate an Innovator in the customer's DMU! Equally, take care about putting your most enthusiastic innovators in front of the customer's 'good solid' Early Majority.

As a matchmaking tool, this one is hard to beat.

Levels of seniority

Don't get stuck at too junior a level, but also don't cause resentment in the ranks by only attending to the bosses. Figure 7.7 suggests the roles taken by different levels of seniority in the customer's organization, so suggesting the nature of the contact and relationship you might be seeking with each.

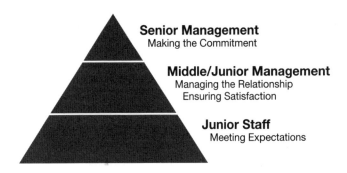

Figure 7.7   *Levels of seniority*

Junior staff have to stick to the rules, while breaking the rules is what makes senior managers senior. Junior staff have targets to meet, while senior managers set those targets. Junior staff are focused on today, while senior management (it is to be hoped) are focused on far beyond tomorrow. Obvious stuff perhaps, but too often suppliers end up having the wrong conversations at the different levels, usually because they have limited the relationship to sales people in pursuit of orders.

The matchmaking process of the value machine requires the supplier to identify the 'wants' and 'needs' of these different levels ('wants' are desires, 'needs' are necessities). Do they correspond or do they conflict at the different levels of seniority? What does this tell you about the nature of the customer's organization? Does it suggest that your propositions might be better suited to one level than another?

Supporters and Opponents

Figure 7.8 aims to plot the members of the customer's DMU based on two considerations:

1.   Do they agree with your business proposition?
2.   Do they have trust and confidence in you as a supplier?

Some interesting things happen when a cross-functional team is gathered to plot the customer contacts in this way. Sometimes they find themselves in violent disagreement, and so the tool has worked on that all-important level – as a vehicle to stimulate debate. Sometimes they find that all the names go into the Supporter box, and yet as a supplier they have less than 10 per cent of the customer's business. So, are they fooling themselves, or are they ignoring a whole chunk of people? Another useful debate.

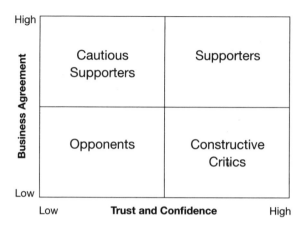

Figure 7.8 *Supporters and opponents*

Avoiding people who neither like your company nor go along with your proposition (Opponents) is of course a very human thing to do, but not something we should allow in a true value machine organization. Opponents are particularly susceptible to what we might call the 'fester-factor'; at best they sulk and gripe (a peculiarly infectious behaviour when seated deep inside a customer), while at worst they may be actively campaigning against you, energetically boosting your competitors – your Opponent may very likely be your competitor's Sponsor (see above). Such people cannot be ignored.

Aim to discover why they have such low trust and confidence in you: is it history, is it personal chemistry, is it a misunderstanding? Then aim to do something about it. Don't try to move Opponents upwards in the matrix before you have moved them rightwards – people who don't trust you won't listen to even the very finest of propositions (a truth not always recognized by all parties in a cross-functional supplier team).

Cautious Supporters are a potential risk – they are effectively waiting for a better option to come along, from a 'better-looking' competitor. Again, aim to understand their reservations and act to remove them.

Constructive Critics can tell you where you are going wrong, which is something that we should be eager to hear, even though they don't agree with our propositions. We might learn more from such people than anyone else in the organization, painful though it may be at the time.

In short, aim to cover all four groups of people and deploy your own team in a way most likely to enhance trust and confidence, so moving each contact rightwards in preparation for the upward movement based on your improved (as a result of all these contacts) value proposition.

Who sits around the table?

Figure 7.9 shows a series of concentric tables, around each of which sit different members of the customer's DMU.

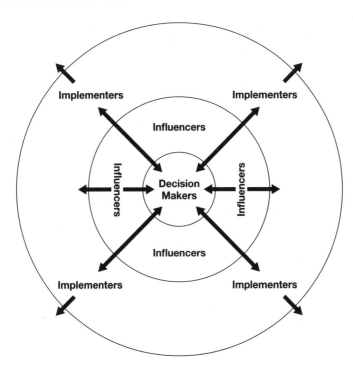

Figure 7.9 *Who sits around the table?*
(with thanks to Steve Lobb)

Around the central table sit the 'Policy Makers' – important people, but it is not enough to focus on them alone. Around the next table sit those that we call 'Influencers', almost certainly a larger group of people. The nature of their influence might be any mixture of the kinds we have been considering throughout this chapter. A third table has a yet larger group of people sitting around its edge – the 'Implementers'.

The arrows remind us that the flow of influences and decisions goes both ways, and it is for the supplier to determine which of those lines they wish to work along, which to develop, and perhaps, in the case of negative messages, which to damp down.

This is not an easy tool to use, in so far as the arguments over who sits where can be endless, but as will be clear by now this is in fact its great value. So often this tool will upset the applecart of accepted wisdom – a true maverick's tool. Gather a cross-functional team, draw the circles on a flipchart, issue everyone with pads of that wonderfully half-sticky yellow paper, asking them to write the names of all their contacts and affix them to the flipchart. Stand back and cue the debate…

A composite tool

The last of the analytical tools in this chapter is an example of a composite, an attempt to put together the data culled from a number of the tools discussed. There are of course as many composites as you choose to create; this is simply an example.

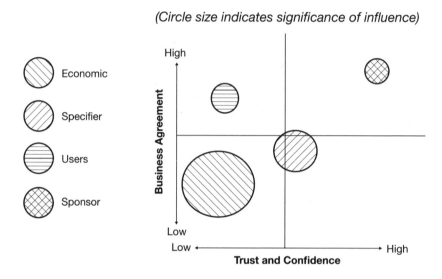

Figure 7.10 *A composite tool*

This composite combines the analysis from:

- the *Supporters and Opponents* matrix (Figure 7.8);
- the *Type of Involvement* analysis (User/Specifier etc, Figure 7.4);
- the *Influencer Matrix* (Figure 7.3).

We might look inside the workings of a particular supplier team, faced with this analysis…

The Economic buyer is clearly a big problem, and there must be a strategy to improve their feelings of trust in the supplier – achieved through something of a 'charm-offensive' by senior management (after much discussion it was recognized that the Economic buyer's low level of trust was due to a long period of inattention from the supplier).

There are allies within the customer's DMU, although the team recognized that they had been putting too much faith in a Sponsor who loved them but was not particularly well regarded.

The Users were very positive about the product they received, but had felt let down by a poor delivery track record – the Account Manager quickly secured the help of the Logistics people in their team to assess the cause and implement a highly advertised improvement plan.

The Specifier was in need of a boost to their confidence in the product, and this was achieved by sending them some detailed reports on its efficacy, drawn up by the supplier's technical service team working alongside the Users.

A repeat analysis was conducted after six months, with the gratifying sight of the circles moving steadily rightward and upwards.

THE ACTION TOOLS

While the analytical tools described are an optional toolkit, the two action tools to which they lead – the Contact Matrix and the G.R.O.W.s – are so important, so valuable, and so fundamental to the management of the value machine that I would like to suggest you regard them as mandatory.

The essence of any collaborative partnership has to be: *who works with whom, and for what purpose*. In Chapter 6 we looked at the range of relationship models, from the Bow-tie to the Diamond Team, recognizing the increasing complexity as we move up the relationship ladder. Here we will detail the tools that allow us to handle this complexity, and further, to develop effective cross-functional teams charged with the task of improving the customer value proposition and also our returns from that enhancement.

The Contact Matrix

It is to be supposed that the matchmaking process with our Key Accounts is aiming to achieve something along the lines of the Diamond Teams described in Chapter 6 (see Figure 6.8). The importance of the Contact Matrix – one of the simplest tools in the whole toolkit, yet perhaps the most important of them all – becomes apparent if we remind ourselves of just one of the challenges of

Diamond Teams: the members work for a variety of functions and a variety of bosses – very few, if any, will respond directly to the Key Account Manager. The result, if not managed effectively, might be chaos, frustration, missed opportunities, overkill or just plain ignorance.

How many people from your organization are in contact with your most important customer? Most are surprised when they start to track the contact points, perhaps uncovering a situation not unlike that shown in Figure 6.9, what we called the relationship to avoid. Of course, worse than not knowing who is in contact is not knowing what they are doing...

The Contact Matrix (Figure 7.11) begins to address this problem.

	Account Manager	Your team member	Your team member	Your team member	Your team member	Your team member
Buying Director	XXX					
Their team member	[XX]		XXX	X		[XX]
Their team member		XXX			X	
Their team member	X			[XXX]		[X]
Their team member						
Their team member	X					[XXX]

Figure 7.11   *The contact matrix*

Whether kept as part of a CRM (customer relationship management) system, or a simple Excel spreadsheet, this should be available to all involved with the customer, as a reference for what is going on around them.

If we look at the example in Figure 7.11 we should be able to come to some fast conclusions, even without any particular knowledge of the customer in question:

- There is one member of the customer team that nobody sees. This is not uncommon in a complex situation where everyone thinks that someone else was handling that one...
- Four people are in contact with one member of the customer's team. Again, not uncommon in a situation where contacts have developed over long periods of time, but is the poor soul being swamped by the supplier, or worse, is the supplier speaking at cross purposes?

- If the number of crosses is used to indicate the importance of a particular contact, and if 'bad' relationships are highlighted in some way (in the example they are shown by the boxed crosses), then there should be some alarms sounding. First, action needs to be taken with the two 'triple-cross' contacts that are showing as poor. Second, a coaching session is long overdue with the team member who has three points of contact, all bad…

The ever changing scene…

Working with a complex customer there may be several DMUs in operation – perhaps separate business units, or locations, or buying processes – and it may become too confusing to try to capture all of this on the one Contact Matrix. Separate matrices are fine, provided you don't lose the big picture – perhaps a grand summary, or 'master matrix' will remain useful.

The Contact Matrix is not a static tool, people come and go, and those changes must be captured by regular reviews. Keep it simple, and the reviews will not be a burden; over-complicate the tool and it will fast become a bureaucratic nightmare. Above all else, adapt this tool to suit your own circumstances.

The G.R.O.W.s

With specific knowledge of the customer, and our own objectives, the Contact Matrix can take us a great deal further. With the addition of G.R.O.W.s the tool becomes the heart of our team and contact management strategy.

For each point of contact we add a G.R.O.W. as shown in Figure 7.12.

	Ken Reilly	Your team member	**Rob Jones**	Your team member	Your team member	Your team member
John Smith	XXX	Ken Reilly – John Smith				
Their team member	XX	G – Secure order for xxxx R – Present solution yyyy O – Brief team on progress	X		XX
Their team member		W – By 7th Aug, London		X	
Paul Knight					
Their team member		Paul Knight – R&D Specifier Early Adopter Cautious supporter Is influenced by…	Rob Jones – Paul Knight G – Develop new market for xxxx R – Deliver training yyyy O – Feedback learning to KA team		
Their team member			W – By 3rd July, Zurich		

Figure 7.12 *The contact matrix with G.R.O.Ws (and DMU information)*

G = Goal   – the overall purpose of the contact;
R = Role   – the activities to be carried out in pursuit of that goal;
O = Obligation   – the responsibilities of the team member to the team and customer;
W = Work Plan – the details of dates and actions.

If we consider two further challenges of working in a Diamond Team, we will see the vital importance of this tool. Many of the members of such teams will be from senior management, with the full range of egos and 'independent behaviours' that this brings. Such people are not easy to control... Each of the members will doubtless aim to operate to what they regard as a high level of excellence, based on the principles of their own function – which can easily lead to conflict between competing definitions of excellence...

The G.R.O.W. aims to handle these two problems, by agreeing the objectives and scope of each contact, and in the context of the wider team. Begin with the 'team G.R.O.W.' – the overall purpose of the relationship – and then agree each individual G.R.O.W. through discussion between the Account Manager and the individual concerned.

This discussion is an important element of the process; don't be tempted to allow the Account Manager to write the G.R.O.W.s – they may do it speedily, but they will come to little. We are attempting to harness a diverse range of talents and working styles, and make of these a single-minded team, and in pursuit of this we should note a few 'rules':

- Specialists will often know better than the Account Manager what they can contribute to the team, and the customer.
- It is the Account Manager's job to extract that contribution, through discussion with the team member, and through coaching.
- People will be more motivated to contribute if they feel they had a hand in deciding their contribution.
- People, particularly those that don't work for the Account Manager, and who may be senior to them, rarely respond well to being 'told' what to do.
- Teams work best when there is a high degree of self-management based on mutual trust; the simple discipline of G.R.O.W.s facilitates such an understanding.

Don't be too short-term with the G.R.O.W.s. If people have to renew them every two weeks then don't expect to see them renewed much more than twice... The timescale should relate to the overall purpose of the relationship, and if we are aiming for a long-term collaborative partnership, perhaps even hoping for the joint development of new products and services, then the nature of the G.R.O.W.s should reflect that.

MATCHING – PROTECTING YOUR INVESTMENT

That a great deal of work is required to use the tools described in this chapter is undeniable, only you can judge the value of the return on the effort put in. They are clearly not for every customer circumstance, but if you have Key or Key Development Accounts, and if you wish to start the matching process of the value machine, then they are almost certainly vital. Any investment should be made based on the best possible intelligence, and these tools aim to provide that from the ground floor up. You wouldn't even think of starting a joint development programme with a customer without knowing their decision-making process, or the identity and roles of the key influencers – would you?

8

The business strategy

The matching process is about being relevant, to the customer and to our own business objectives. First we must involve the relevant people on both sides – that was the focus of Chapter 7. Then we must aim to work on the relevant issues – this will be the focus of the present chapter. Finally we must come up with the relevant value proposition – and that will be the focus of Chapter 9.

So, how might we define the relevant issues: are they those things that the customer demands from us? Might that not simply put us into the hands of unscrupulous buyers? A better angle will be to understand something of the customer's business strategy; not the whole detail, but enough to identify the key drivers, to speak the right language, and to ensure that our thoughts resonate with theirs.

We are talking of matching the customer's business strategy, but don't think that means we have to have the same strategy in our own business – that would rather limit our choice of customers! Much as in life, opposites can attract: the key to the value machine's matching process is to be found in being relevant, not in being the same.

KEY SUPPLIER STATUS – THE BUYER'S AGENDA

As in the last chapter, let us begin with the purchasing professionals. If we are not on the buyer's radar we will be hard pressed to form the kind of relationships necessary to the value machine. So why should they let you in? Why should they allow you access beyond their own function? What benefit do they see in the forming of a Diamond Team? Why should they abandon some of the 'sharper' tactics in the professional buyer's book of tricks by letting you 'realize' your true value? First, there are plenty of reasons why they should *not*:

- they might regard such relationships as a 'weapon' used by suppliers in order to secure greater power and influence in the negotiation;
- they might lose the benefits of 'dividing and ruling' a disorganized supplier;
- they might value an individual contact (the sales rep) more than they do the company;
- they might see you as 'muscling in' on their market;
- it might not suit the way that they buy;
- they don't regard you as a Key Supplier.

All might be true, but the last is the most damaging of them all. We must begin then by understanding their definitions and *positioning* of suppliers.

Buyers have come a long way in the last few years – the impact of IT has been significant, as has the realization that purchasing can make a significant difference not only to the bottom line but also to the success of the business strategy. For a 'good' supplier, that is, one with genuine value to offer, the changes make for good news in the main:

- buyers are more involved in the business processes, often as a part of cross-functional sourcing teams, so promising you greater access to others if your contribution is a positive one;
- buyers are more concerned with the longer term – short-term gains based on price have been seen too many times to be damaging to the health of their business;
- buyers are measured on their impact on the business, not simply on their ability to get price reductions;
- buyers' knowledge of their own business, rather than the product they buy, has improved significantly;
- the buyer's assessment of their suppliers has grown more sophisticated, based on ideas of cost and value in use;
- buyers have greater knowledge of their suppliers – not only what they buy, but the nature and capabilities of those suppliers;
- the buyer as stubborn gatekeeper is perhaps a fading figure – they are encouraged to facilitate access to the business, but only for those suppliers that will make a positive contribution as a result, not for suppliers simply after a quick buck...

If a supplier understands these changes, and is willing to respond, it can be very good news indeed, but they will need to reassess some old notions of the 'balance of power'. For many years there was an approximate equality of power between suppliers and customers, often the result of an equal ignorance of the other's true situation. The new purchasing behaviours, and the buyer's greatly enhanced knowledge of their own business requirements and the potential of their suppliers – what we might call a purchasing revolution – has shifted that balance of power significantly in their favour. For suppliers, attempts to arm-wrestle over the negotiating table are likely to bring poorer returns than attempts to collaborate.

SUPPLY CHAIN MANAGEMENT

Supply Chain Management (SCM) used to be seen principally as a means of reducing costs. By removing unnecessary steps from the chain of activities – from procurement through to sales – money could be saved. Buyers were keen to be involved in this process.

As time passed and unnecessary costs were removed, a second objective arose: speeding the chain through smooth and flawless execution. Buyers were also keen to be involved in this process.

More latterly a third objective has been added, and is now perhaps the most dominant; focusing all internal activities on improving the value of the final offer to the customer. Buyers of the new stamp have been keen to be involved in this pursuit, and to the benefit of those suppliers that have value both *inside* and *beyond* the business.

Value inside and beyond

Where does your value actually register? Figure 8.1 illustrates the notion of registering 'inside' the customer, or 'beyond'.

While it might at first appear that value inside the customer is more important, registering more immediately and obviously with the customer, we should remember what most customers are: businesses, just like our own. And what is most important to a business? Pleasing their customers. If we are in the happy position of providing value to our customers' customers then we *should* be enjoying the rewards of our benefits. To be sure of our reward we will need to be sure of our value, and this will very likely require us to be in contact with the people to whom this value matters, the people responsible for taking the supply chain into the customer's customer – perhaps the marketing team, maybe logistics, almost certainly the sales force.

Value
'inside' the
customer

= cost reduction
= process improvement
= waste reduction,
  etc...

Value
'beyond' the
customer

= quality improvement
= price increase
= market development,
  etc...

Figure 8.1 *Value inside, or beyond the customer?*

A company sells different types and grades of paper used in the packaging industry. The immediate customer is the 'converter'; the company that takes the paper, and other products, and turn it into finished packaging, whether it be a humble soap powder carton, or a glossy box for an upmarket perfume. Figure 8.2 shows the different markets into which the converter sells.

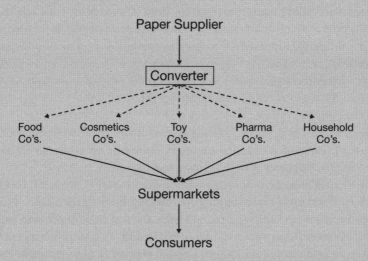

Figure 8.2 *The packaging chain*

I once worked with such a paper supplier that denied they had any need to 'independently' understand the market beyond the converter, as the converter would tell them all that they needed to know, case by case. If they had meant that their aim was to understand the markets 'in partnership' with the converter, then I would have been happier, but unfortunately what they meant was that it was easiest just to do as they were told.

This was of course a buyer's paradise, for the buyer chose to tell them only what they saw as useful in the negotiation. 'Our market is driven by cost,' they said, citing the household goods customers as their example. So much was true, but what they didn't say was the range of other values that mattered to other customers: the food companies requiring high standards of hygiene; the perfume and cosmetic manufacturers concerned principally with image; the toy producers looking for safety above all else; the garden chemicals companies eager to see longevity and durability.

So, costs were driven downwards, and the supplier was steadily commoditized. When the buyer had them lying prostrate on the floor, they delivered their next set of demands: we need paper that will improve hygiene levels, allow products to 'glow in the dark', be non-toxic, and super-tear-resistant…

So the supplier works on those new value propositions, but, from their position as a commoditized and downtrodden supplier of paper, and they never quite managed to achieve their just rewards – as a supplier of packaging solutions.

Buyers negotiate on price because it is simple, because they have the advantage of knowing the range of offers from all competitors (while the individual supplier may only know their own), and because plenty of suppliers, it would seem, are all too ready to offer discounts rather than work harder to discover their true value.

A buyer prepared to work harder, and with the help of a good supplier, will be open to discussions over 'cost in use' or lifetime value. This is where the price is regarded as only one element of the costs to the customer; there are also the costs of storage, of physically using the product, of servicing or replacement, as well as plenty of other elements to consider. It is quite common for the supplier with the lowest selling price to cause the customer the highest costs in those other areas, and a calculation of the total 'cost in use' might show them up for not being quite the bargain they seemed.

Of course, for a premium-priced supplier to gain any advantage from this kind of analysis they must not only understand the nature of their cost in use, but also be able to calculate it on behalf of the buyer. Buyers may have come a long way, but they still don't go out of their way to find work. And if a cost in use advantage is found not to exist, then they may be wise to develop one – this of course is the value machine in action.

A manufacturer of heavy-duty electric pumps has just learned that their long-term price of €40,000 is being undercut by a new supplier offering a similar pump for €36,000. Their largest customer is seriously considering switching as they see no advantages in the €40,000 pump.

The incumbent supplier does some research on the new supplier and finds them to be reputable, and with an excellent pump – much the same specification, and unfortunately using the same amount of energy – no cost in use advantage to be found there...

They might give up at that point and reduce their price to match, or they might do some further research into the nature of the customer's usage, research they should of course have done already, but it is amazing what a little competition does for a supplier.

Making use of contacts within the customer's supply chain they discover that over a five-year period the pump that costs €40,000 to buy, costs the customer an additional €230,000 in energy. The competitor's pump will cost just the same, so still no advantage, but the discovery spurs an idea.

This is a Key Customer, and remembering the principles of the value machine they realize that an investment is long overdue. The sales team approach their R&D colleagues with a simple question: is it possible to develop a new pump with a 10 per cent improvement in energy consumption? Of course, everything is possible, but at a cost. Time for some calculations: to cover the cost of investment the pump will need to be sold for €44,000, but a 10 per cent saving on energy over five years is worth €23,000 per installation – so the premium of €8,000 over the competitor's pump is easily justified.

But the supplier was not home and dry. R&D had only said it was possible, that's not the same as them starting work – by what authority, to what budget? That's the internal hurdle.

The buyer only buys pumps, not energy, so why should they care? That's the customer hurdle.

Of course, they have come to this rather the wrong way around; trying to solve a customer problem before organizing the internal team, and without involving the customer so as to pave the way for the value proposition. Value doesn't just exist – it has to be communicated.

Fortunately there is a happy ending. The Leadership Team is engaged to authorize the work, and a Sales/R&D Key Account Team is set up to manage the customer communication. It all takes a little longer than it might have done, and it is unlikely, even at €44,000, that they will recoup the investment with this customer, but it is now that the real benefit of the value machine kicks in. After a short period of exclusivity with the original customer the supplier can now offer the new pump to all of their customers. Their enhanced value proposition now starts to pay off handsomely.

Had this supplier had their time again they would of course have done their research earlier, and spoken with the customer earlier to understand their concerns (if they had any) regarding energy costs. Most importantly, they would have managed the relationship better in order to identify and communicate the value they were about to deliver.

Figure 8.3 illustrates the supply chain (much simplified) in a hospital, as it exists to source, receive, manage and use surgical instruments.

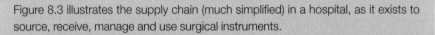

Figure 8.3 *The hospital 'supply chain'*

A particular supplier of surgical instruments, in pursuit of competitive advantage in a market that has become focused on price is launching a new product – the 'procedure pack'. This new idea aims to do the customer's thinking for them, delivering a complete pack of all the items required for any particular operation, or 'procedure'. It has several advantages over the old method of selling instruments as individual items, and not least the question of safety at the point of use – there being no risk of the surgeon finding themselves without an important instrument at a vital moment.

They present it to the buyer, who rejects it. All the buyer sees are premium-priced products, gathered together in a box instead of sold individually. It is clear to the supplier that their value exists 'beyond' the buyer, with those who physically move or manage or use the instruments, but that the decision is resolutely stuck in the hands of a 'gatekeeping' buyer (see Chapter 7).

Fortunately, this supplier is versed in the principles of the value machine and is up to the challenge. They set about understanding the nature of their value beyond the buyer, as shown in Figure 8.4.

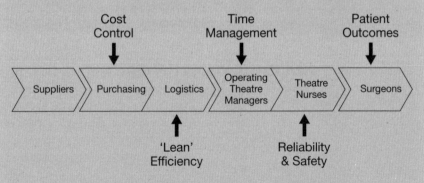

Figure 8.4 *The nature of value in the supply chain*

Now comes the choice; which value to pick on? In theory, the intensity of the supplier's value increases as we move to the right-hand side of the chain – saving lives is 'more valuable' than smoothing the path of the logistics people. But this is 'in theory'. What if there have been no incidents 'in practice' suggesting any kind of problem with the old method of sourcing? What does this theory mean in any case to a buyer expected to save money from a shrinking budget and who is focused on financial measures of performance?

The supplier chooses to focus on the value brought to the operating theatre manager – the procedure pack saves them time, often as much as 40 minutes per operation. Everyone knows that 'time means money' and so a value proposition can be put to the buyer in their own language. Better still, the proposition is not made by the supplier's sales people, but by the operating theatre managers, armed with the time-saving benefit as briefed by the supplier and appealing to their own buyers to source this new 'valuable solution'.

Sometimes an enhanced value proposition will be suggested by the buyer, and suppliers asked to bid. Such customer-inspired initiatives are perhaps easier to make happen within the supplier's organization – customer demands usually weigh heavier than home-grown suggestions (and more the pity for that) – but the rewards may be less.

A typical example is the drive for 'lean supply'. Non-value-added activities are removed from the chain by outsourcing them to existing suppliers. Some suppliers might see this as an additional burden for which they might receive little compensation, others might see an opportunity to bind themselves more closely to the customer: the much sought after *lock-in*.

In making their decision the supplier should always try to consider the less obvious advantages – by extending their involvement with the customer they will undoubtedly see more and learn more; a good position from which to identify further (and supplier initiated) enhancements to the value proposition.

SUPPLIER POSITIONING

Suppliers that are unable to demonstrate their relevance are denied time and access. Buyers prefer to spend their time with suppliers that matter, and they often go to some lengths to ensure that they can distinguish between the former and the latter. Anyone who has heard their customer speaking of a 'supply base optimization' programme is probably already working with a buyer that has gone through this 'supplier positioning' process.

There are a number of models used in such exercises, mostly based on a four-box matrix, each using different words, or adding to the confusion by labelling the sides of the matrix in diametrically opposite ways to their fellows, but they mostly come from the same 'parent' – the Kraljic Matrix.

Figure 8.5 shows a typical variant of the 'Kraljic', one that I have encountered more often 'in practice' than the 'parent', and also having the benefit of using a language more resonant to suppliers.

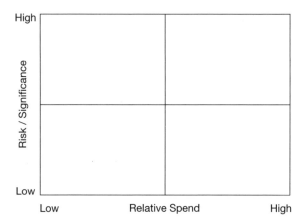

Figure 8.5 *The supplier positioning matrix*
Developed from the Kraljic matrix

The horizontal axis positions suppliers by the proportion of spend, whether as a proportion of their total purchases, or more likely in relation to a particular product category, or perhaps (in the more sophisticated manifestations) as a proportion of the total costs of one of the customer's own finished products. The variations are as many as you care to consider, so it is wise to be sure of how your buyer works before jumping to any fast conclusions!

The vertical axis is rather more subjective, assessing the relative significance of each supplier, and that could be down to a wide range of criteria. Some buyers prefer to use the word 'risk' rather than 'significance', expressing a concept well known to purchasing professionals but somewhat less appreciated elsewhere: the more significant a supplier is to the customer the more risk is taken by granting them large amounts of business. What if they let you down? What if they go bust? It should be no surprise that buyers are not particularly keen on having too many 'significant' suppliers.

The following is a general list of the sort of factors (and is by no means exhaustive) that might be used in this 'significance' or 'risk' analysis:

- the number of suppliers;
- geographic location – distant suppliers might imply greater risk;

- dependence on a particular technology or type of solution – are their alternatives?
- the criticality of their product to our own product/process;
- supplier brand names or trade marks used by the customer – Intel has a great significance to many a PC manufacturer;
- patents, copyrights;
- are the suppliers also competitors?
- do the suppliers work with our competitors?
- the amount of time required to switch suppliers – if it takes a day, they're not that significant, if it takes a year, then they have a significant hold over us… ;
- the supplier's financial stability;
- politics – are they the MD's favourite…?
- the existence of contracts.

Having mapped out the suppliers across the matrix, the buyer might then aim to use the analysis for any or all of the following:

- to decide where to spend their time;
- to decide the nature of the relationship with different 'supplier types' (each box in the matrix contains a different 'supplier type');
- to determine their expectations from each different 'supplier type';
- to identify the type of activities to be engaged in with different 'supplier types';
- to identify where it is necessary to 'develop supplier capabilities';
- to consider options such as 'open-book trading';
- to manage risk;
- to determine the right sort of contract;
- to identify their 'Key Suppliers'.

Managing suppliers

Figure 8.6 shows the kind of labels that might be applied to the four 'supplier types' in the supplier positioning matrix.

Each of these supplier types carries a set of guidelines for the buying team, based on the following broad questions:

- How much time should we spend with them?
- What type of relationship do we require/will we allow?
- What are our expectations?
- How will improvements be managed?
- Must we reduce our risk, and how?
- How will we behave – collaboratively or competitively?

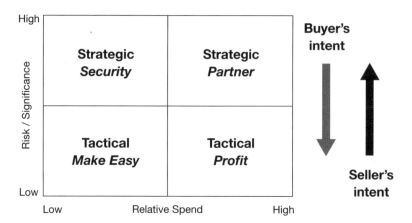

Figure 8.6 *Supplier types*

These might be some 'typical' summaries by type:

Tactical *Make Easy* – such suppliers don't deserve much time or attention and the relationship should be as simple as possible, perhaps even 'electronically managed'. Ideally the supplier will be largely self-managing (any supplier that proves difficult to work with is a dead supplier), and those who can take on broad responsibilities may even be granted sole supplier arrangements.

Tactical *Profit* – we will spend such time as is appropriate in securing the best financial outcome, preferring a simple one-on-one relationship where we have the advantage of knowledge. A steady improvement in price and terms is required, and there is a choice of encouraging competition between suppliers (regular rotation of suppliers is an acceptable tactic) or promising steady volume increases to a few in return for steady discounting.

Strategic *Security* – time will be spent if it contributes to security and consistency of supply but we place a big responsibility on suppliers to manage this for us. We will intervene if we think they need our help. Relationships will be open, allowing supplier access where it is important to our main objective. We will continually look for alternatives, as a means to reducing our risk, but will work collaboratively with those suppliers who realize our potential dependence and do not seek to exploit their position. Price is not a significant issue, but we expect suppliers to take on a good deal of responsibility for managing improvements in return for this 'privilege'.

Strategic *Partner* – this is where we plan to spend most time, with a long-term relationship facilitating cross-functional links (the 'Diamond Team'). We expect a lot from these suppliers – continually improving value propositions – but also recognize our own responsibility in managing this process. We will collaborate if they allow us a role in managing their improvement programmes – joint investment is a possible approach, we may give guarantees of future business if this facilitates the supplier's investment, and we may even be interested in such things as training supplier staff in critical skills to help them meet our standards and reduce our risk.

Through the 1980s and 1990s, Marks & Spencer led the way in managing their strategic partners to the point that those suppliers thought, talked and acted like Marks & Spencer – true synergy. Some suppliers became very reliant on Marks & Spencer, put their trust in the customer's judgement, and allowed the customer to determine their ranges, quality standards, service levels, even their margins.

Was this good for suppliers? Many benefited enormously, but when hard times hit M&S in 1999 many of these symbiotic links were broken, with damaging consequences for those suppliers that had become dependent (perhaps over-dependent?).

Close management of suppliers, in the way once practised by M&S, can gain much in the way of control and efficiency, but it also implies a risk, in this case the risk of losing an 'independent' supplier's flair and innovation. Much of the retailer's woes in those years can be put down to a kind of cloning that went on between customer and supplier. When a customer takes on all the responsibility for things such as their supplier's product development, then they just have to get it right because there isn't anyone else to come up with the ideas. A successful relationship in this box must recognize the potential perils as well as the benefits of such closeness – only then can it guard against them.

A supplier has a unique and critical ingredient in a big-brand consumer food product. It accounts for less than half a per cent of total expenditure on the materials for the final product. This is a 'top-left' strategic security supplier with a vengeance. Margins are good (no buyer is going to risk supply of such a product by switching to another supplier for the sake of a 5 per cent discount), and they have a long-term contract as a sole supplier. In return they give exclusivity, and 100 per cent reliability and consistency are assured.

This situation has maintained for many years and from the buyer's perspective has always been seen as a big risk – being so dependent in such a critical area (what some buyers would call a 'bottleneck' item) – but they were stuck with an arrangement that had been established by their R&D colleagues more years ago than anyone could remember...

One day, the supplier had problems with their own supply base and failed to deliver. Everyone blamed the buyer for the fact that the production line was halted, and then worse, the next batch, made in a hurry, was out of spec and an emergency product recall was instituted.

121

The supplier made much of the fact that this was the first such instance in over eight years, but for the anxious buyer once was enough and they seized control. There were to be no more sole-supplier arrangements, indeed no supplier was to have more than 50 per cent of the business, and the incumbent supplier would have to give their recipe to the new competitors.

MATCHING – BEING RELEVANT – RAISING OUR STATUS

The positioning of suppliers through something like the Kraljic Matrix is of course a very similar process to that of the K.A.I.S.M. described in Chapter 5, though its mirror image: classifying suppliers rather than classifying customers. Its similarity should suggest something important however – we are not so different from customers as we often suppose. We are both in pursuit of 'partners' where we can match our capabilities with other's ambitions – we are both in fact part of the same value machine, if only we can identify our relevance to each other.

The best way to be relevant to a customer, over the long term, is to make a positive impact on their business strategy. The rest of this chapter will explore a number of tools for checking and matching that strategy. The discussion so far in this chapter has been regarding the customer's purchasing strategy, a sub-set of the business strategy but a vital one for a very simple reason: if we fail to be appropriate to their expectations at this point in the relationship we are unlikely to make much meaningful progress elsewhere.

Let's conclude our discussion of the buyer's strategy with a typical problem: what if the buyer regards us as less significant than the rest of their own organization does, what if we feel wrongly positioned, what if we need to raise our status in order to achieve our goals for and with the customer?

The task of raising your status must begin by being appropriate to your current status – buyers can often be harder on suppliers who behave 'above their status' than those that fall below.

Next, start building relationships beyond the buyer, utilizing your full supplier team as appropriate, while always seeking the buyer's advice and permission and always keeping them informed.

Make sure you understand the way in which the buyer is measured. You may think that they don't care about the supply chain, or value with their own customers, but that may only be because they have positioned you 'below the line'. With suppliers in the two 'strategic' boxes, 'above the line', the conversations may be very different.

Stretch the buyer's horizons. If they are interested in cost in use, then aim to make it a _real_ interest; offer to do studies for them, make the calculations for them, and communicate the results to those that need to know.

Finally, start to show how you make an impact on their broader business strategy through identifying their problems and providing appropriate solutions – which brings us to the next part of this chapter.

STRATEGIC SUPPLIER STATUS – THE BUSINESS STRATEGY AGENDA

This is about going beyond benefits and looking for real solutions to real business problems. It goes beyond the pursuit of key supplier status; we are aiming here for _strategic supplier status_. We will ask four questions of the customer's business strategy:

1. How do they plan to grow?
2. How do they plan to compete?
3. What makes them excel?
4. What is their money-making logic?

The answers will not give us a full assessment of their business strategy (there is plenty more to know), but they will tell us enough to know our value, and to assess our ability to enhance that value in pursuit of a collaborative relationship.

Two competitors are each trying to sell an x-ray machine to a private hospital. One costs £400,000, the other £550,000, and they apparently do much the same job.

The buyer, an old-fashioned type with no time for supplier positioning models, calls it a 'no brainer' and goes for the cheaper machine. They feel happy with a good day's work that saved the hospital £150,000.

Over the next two years the x-ray machine is serviced eight times, each time at a cost of £10,000, plus it required a major overhaul costing £20,000. Oddly enough, the buyer doesn't care; they are not responsible for servicing costs, which come out of the radiology department's budget.

The machine has broken down on two occasions, resulting in major patient log-jams, a lot of ill-will towards the hospital and one very expensive court case for negligence. Oddly enough, the buyer doesn't care; they are not responsible for patient-processing targets and they rarely go to court or read the newspapers.

A competing hospital in the next town bought the more expensive x-ray machine. The service contract requires only two services a year, each at £5,000, and the machine has never broken down. The hospital has no patient log-jams, and no bad press.

They are doing well, and stealing patients from the hospital with the cheaper machine and the PR problems. Not surprisingly, people want to go to the hospital that isn't in the newspapers.

This case is all about value, but of two rather different types. The first is the type of value that saves the customer money – lower servicing costs that make the more expensive machine the better buy in the long run. Attractive and interesting, but there are things yet more attractive and interesting to a customer. How about defending the hospital's reputation?

I once heard a hospital manager say: 'If the customers feel they can trust us then they don't begrudge having more expensive coffee in the waiting room. They don't even mind if they have to pay for things that other hospitals do for free – but do badly.'

The supplier that helps the hospital meet their strategic objectives – in this case building trust with the public – will more than likely be regarded as a strategic supplier.

How do they plan to grow?

The real question is of course the supplementary one: *and do we help them?*

The Ansoff Matrix, shown in Figure 8.7, illustrates the four growth options open to us all, if we reckon that growth will come from any combination of existing or new products (vertical axis) sold into existing or new markets (horizontal axis).

Figure 8.7 *The Ansoff matrix*

The percentage figures are illustrative of the likely success rate of each of the four strategies, or put another way, they show that risk increases as we move around the matrix from *Penetration* (selling more of the existing products into existing markets) to *Market Extension* (selling existing products into new markets) to *New Product Development* (selling new products into existing markets) and on to *Diversification* (selling new products into new markets).

Our analytical task is to identify the nature of the customer's growth strategy, and so assess the level of risk involved. This could lead us in either of two main directions; deciding to work with those customers that take the lowest risks and so have the greatest chance of success – effectively riding on the back of their success – or, aiming to help customers reduce their risks.

We might do rather nicely from the first of these choices, provided that their success is spectacular enough, but our contribution to that success will have been limited and we will not be expecting any premium reward.

The second choice involves ourselves in a measure of risk, but as with any higher risk investment the payout is likely to be better if we both succeed.

In the context of the value machine, and when working alongside our key customers, it is the second of the two investment strategies that is likely to interest us most; aiming to improve our customer's chances of success, and through close collaboration (so that they are fully aware of our contribution) ensure an attractive return for ourselves.

Our approach and potential contribution will of course differ depending on the growth strategy chosen by the customer.

Penetration – their risks are relatively low and they will more likely be looking for better prices than the development of new value propositions. If their growth is particularly fast however, then the provision of efficient and reliable logistics will certainly be regarded as a plus.

I recall once being rather proud of the fact that a retail customer of mine with spectacular growth plans always chose my company as the most preferred supplier for each new store opening. I put it down to the strength of our brand. It was interesting to learn some years later that the true value we had been bringing was that we had the most reliable logistics in the industry and they could guarantee an on-time opening with our help. On hearing this I was inclined at first to feel a little less proud, and then realized that my pride was well placed, only for the wrong reasons! If only I had known the truth, I could have helped them more, and done rather better out of the arrangements for my own company...

Market Extension – suppliers that can demonstrate knowledge and experience of the customer's new markets will be well placed. They will be more than just suppliers, they have the potential to be 'guides and consultants'. Providing market research data, warning of pitfalls, pointing out unexpected opportunities, perhaps even 'loaning' experienced staff: all of these things will be appreciated, and should be 'rewarded'. That is not to say you can automatically demand a premium price, nor that you send them an invoice for the research. Rewards can be subtler, and in the longer term even more attractive, such as first option and early involvement on new projects, access to key people, higher than normal shares of business, and so on.

New Product Development – creativity, an ability to collaborate with confidentiality, and speed, these are the three most valued supplier contributions to a customer growing through NPD. We might add financial support as a fourth, but although it might occupy more of the discussion time than the other things, it is probably not as important to the customer. Look at it this way; the customer may well proceed without your financial support, and you may both succeed well enough, but if your products fail, or if your loose tongue allows a competitor to steal a march, or if (and worst of all) you bring their timetable to a halt, then don't expect the relationship to continue happily.

The secret of most NPD is speed to market and any supplier seen to slow them down will be in trouble. We can see at this point how the nature of the relationship itself can be represented as something of value to the customer. Imagine a customer dealing with a vital supplier through a Bow-tie relationship (see Figure 6.4). How do they view their supplier in terms of their speed? Figure 8.8, turning the Bow-tie on its side, suggests the answer.

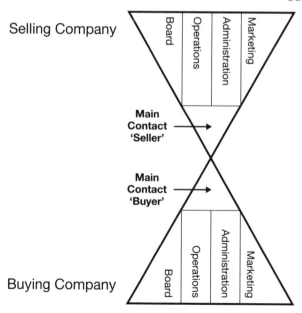

Figure 8.8 *The 'hourglass' or 'log-jam' relationship*

From the customer's perspective it feels like the sand draining through an hourglass – regular enough, but as slow as watching paint dry. The Diamond relationship on the other hand (see Figure 6.8) is far more likely to impress them by providing fast access to the people that can make things happen for them.

Diversification – at the risk of a quick answer that might wrongly suggest that this one is easy, the customer, quite simply, wants it all. Any supplier that can give them efficiency, knowledge, experience, creativity, speed, access to the right people, and perhaps even financial support, will be high on the list of important suppliers. Succeeding with such customers can bring the best returns of all – long-term loyalty, and plenty of invaluable kudos when speaking with other clients.

The importance of matching the customer's aspirations is paramount in this scenario. If you bore them with your ability to deliver three times a week, and offer them extended credit provided they don't ask for any short-notice services, then you should not be surprised if shown the door.

Sir Richard Branson gives some very clear advice to the company pursuing the diversification course, and he should know, having taken Virgin through more diversifications than most (record label to airline to cola manufacturer to personal equity plan seller to mobile phones... etc) and with significantly more success than Ansoff's analysis would suggest. The secret?

- do more market research than anyone thinks is necessary;
- have a brand that acts as a 'halo' around each new activity;
- work with the best and most expert suppliers.

Partnerships are key to Virgin. Virgin brings the brand name; the supplier brings the appropriate expertise. The supplier is expected to take on a good deal of the risk (in some cases, the majority) and should they fail in any way then Virgin retains the right to step in.

Matching the product lifecycle

Nothing lasts forever, growth in particular, and the strategic supplier must always be conscious of the need to change with the times. Figure 8.9 shows a standard product lifecycle moving from *development* to *introduction*, ratcheting up into *growth*, on into *maturity*, *saturation*, and finally *decline*.

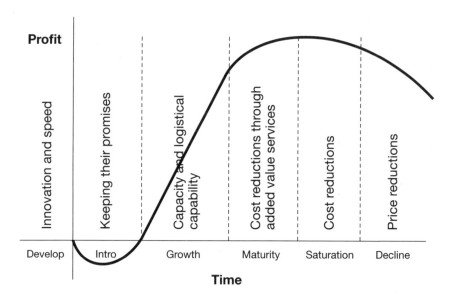

Figure 8.9 The Product Lifecycle and supplier requirements

At each stage of the customer's PLC they will value a different set of activities and contributions from their suppliers, and an alert supplier will find themselves matchmaking with a different set of customer contacts based on those interests.

At the *development* stage it is the involvement of the supplier's R&D team with the customer's R&D and Marketing people, with the focus on speed, creativity and confidential collaboration. At *introduction* a supplier must keep its promises. At *growth*, and particularly if it outpaces the customer's expectations, suppliers that are able to keep up will be welcomed – the logistics team on both sides may come to prominence here. *Maturity* is of course to be avoided if possible, and suppliers bringing ideas and innovations that will breathe new life into an old product will be the first in the queue for attention. The best suppliers don't wait to be asked, nor do they wait for maturity itself – their proposals should perhaps be aired in the right customer quarters even before the growth stage is properly under way. If maturity is unavoidable, the suppliers who can work on supply chain cost-reduction programmes will be favoured. If a product moves into the *decline* phase then very likely the buyer's voice will be the loudest – price reductions being the order of the day.

How do they plan to compete?

As with the customer's growth plans it is the supplementary question that matters; not only: how do they plan to compete? – but also: and do we help them?

Many still accept the 'law' of Michael Porter that there are two principle strategies for gaining competitive advantage: being the lowest-cost supplier, or being a differentiated supplier. Success can result from either strategy, as can failure; the key is in the ability to focus the whole business on whichever route is chosen. A suboptimal outcome usually results when a business vacillates between the two – becoming an 'in-betweeny' – or where there are tensions between key functions, pulling in opposite directions through their allegiance to different strategies.

The budding Strategic Supplier has several tasks to perform here: aim to support the chosen strategy, work to facilitate alignment _within_ the customer, and avoid becoming entrapped in the politics of the customer's internal debates. No easy task. If the customer suffers from the sin of unaligned functions then the task is harder still – which strategy are we trying to match and support? One thing is for sure – such a customer is clearly far from being a value machine.

Helping them to be the lowest-cost supplier

This isn't what you might think – don't confuse this with being 'cheap', or the lowest priced, nor that they will inevitably demand the lowest prices from their suppliers. An expert practitioner of this strategy once said to me: 'the trick is to be the lowest-cost supplier, but not to let the market know!' Targeting the lowest costs means working on the supply chain, and we have seen already in this chapter how that can be an opportunity for a supplier with the right value propositions.

Suppliers who reduce their prices will of course be welcome, but in the end the customer recognizes this for the lazy approach that it is. The real value proposition would be one that helps the customer with their investment in the right capabilities – cost-reducing capabilities.

Lowest cost is more often achieved through investment than disinvestment, particularly if it is to be sustainable lowest cost. The increasing success of Chinese and Indian chemical manufacturers is a case in point. They achieve their remarkably low costs through investing in state of the art technology (something that many of their Western counterparts have fought shy of for years), not the stereotype of cheap labour and unsafe working conditions.

Suppliers that can help with such investments, or suppliers that can reduce their customer's costs through the provision of products and services with superior performance, will almost certainly stand more chance of being regarded as strategic than those who simply offer low prices.

> The easyJet and Ryanair phenomenon is based on a lowest-cost strategy. By operating uniform fleets, flying out of smaller airports with fast turnarounds, keeping their planes in the air for longer, and yes, the no frills approach to service (Michael O'Leary, boss of Ryanair, once called customer service the 'work of the devil') they keep their costs down, but there is one other very important ingredient – the booking system. No middlemen, and an amazingly high proportion of booking through the internet. Do you imagine that when these airlines went out to source a provider for their internet booking system that they went looking for the cheapest? Not at all – a value supplier was one that offered them the very best, providing them with the capability to follow their lowest-cost strategy.

Helping them to be a differentiated supplier

The methods of differentiation are almost endless: product quality, product portfolio, brand image, service provision, staff, location, breadth of distribution, focus of distribution, attitude, style, new product development, social statements, and plenty more. The matching task is one to be performed with some precision in such cases.

Consider a company that wishes to develop a value machine business strategy as its means of differentiation. They seek help from a training provider. Will they choose a provider that suggests the use of an off-the-shelf and on-line training package because it will cut the costs of travel associated with sales training, or will they choose a provider that will work closely to tailor the training to the specific needs? My own company knows the answer to that one, and in cases where the customer has the wrong answer (and yes, customers *can* have the wrong answers) we either aim to change their minds or beat a hasty retreat. There is no sense in aiming to match with a customer when you know they are chasing up the wrong tree. To the right answer we would pull out all the stops, knowing that our capabilities provide the perfect match to their ambitions.

What makes them excel?

I recently sat through a client's boardroom 'debate' as to what mattered most in their business; one said, 'It's what makes us excel that we should be focusing on', while another countered with, 'Oh no, it's what drives us that matters'. I think you will allow they were talking about the same thing?

I mention this only because discussions of this sort can often be rather esoteric, obtuse, over-intellectualized, and sometimes about as useful as a bird of prey with a squint. For a supplier trying to understand their customer, and respond with relevant value, the level of confusion can be significant as different senior managers share their personally favoured models and terminologies. All of this is a great shame, as a clear definition of what makes a company excel, or of what drives it, can be of huge benefit to all concerned.

I strongly recommend the following model and terminology, for its clarity, for its ability to cross business types and functions, and for its simplicity.

M Treacy and F Wiersema, in their book _The Discipline of Market Leaders_, identify three key 'value drivers' present in any successful business, and go on to argue that in really successful businesses, one or other of these drivers tends to stand out, a beacon for their staff, their investors, their suppliers, and for their customers:

- Operational Excellence.
- Product Leadership.
- Customer Intimacy.

Operational Excellence is about doing what you do well. It is about effective processes, smooth mechanics, and the efficiency with which products or services are brought to market. Businesses driven by 'O.E.' will look to suppliers that can enhance uniformity and conformance, improve inventory management, who know about supply chain management, have accurate forecasting systems, slick logistics and unfailing standards.

Product Leadership is about producing the best, leading-edge, or market-dominant products. Investment in NPD will be high and a nagging fear of falling behind leads to a continual pushing at the boundaries of performance. Businesses driven by 'P.L.' will look to suppliers that bring innovation, that are able to work in collaborative partnerships, are willing to share intellectual property, and know how important a thing is 'speed to market'.

Customer Intimacy is the ability to identify with specific customer needs and match products and services accordingly. They have a determination to develop close customer relationships and act on the subsequent knowledge at all levels of their operation. Businesses driven by 'C.I.' will look to suppliers that can enhance those relationships, perhaps through expertise in the market, a flexible responsiveness to subtle changes in customer requirements, or perhaps an ability to work on short specialist runs.

These three short summaries are of course broad generalizations, and the particular expectations from suppliers might differ markedly, but there is at least one certainty: any 'good value idea' from a supplier that fails to make a positive impact on the customer's priority value driver is likely to be viewed as an average or mediocre idea at best, or perhaps just plain irrelevant.

Earlier we discussed the problem of a customer where functions disagreed over the source of their competitive advantage – disagreements over the important value drivers are yet more common, and for an easy-to-see reason. Individual functions can have a tendency to favour those drivers closest to their own 'natural state'. Ask a production team what drives the business and don't be surprised if they say Operational Excellence with no hesitation at all. Ask the R&D folk and the answer may be Product Leadership, and given with just as much certainty. Ask the sales and marketing people and Customer Intimacy is top of the list. So who is right?

If you are dealing with an individual function then you have the ease of being able to take them at their word, but the moment your value proposition begins to impact beyond that individual function you have a problem on your hands.

Suppliers are often able to see the clashes that result from function-specific drivers more readily than the customer. They can see that the customer-intimate sales force is promising product and service variations that are in open conflict with the folk in production and distribution, driven by operational excellence.

Perhaps this is simply an opportunity to help the customer, as a truly strategic supplier – don't forget that they are probably as frustrated by the internal clashes as you are! A good (and politically wise) start is to note that the fault is rarely with the people concerned, but with the way that the chosen value drivers are translated into performance targets.

If the business truly wishes to be customer intimate, then the measures used to assess the contribution of the production folk will have to change, perhaps focusing on their flexibility rather than their occupacity. This allows the production people to take a customer-intimate focus while still being able to use an operationally excellent means of measuring performance – so much better than expecting production to be measured by something as 'distant' as 'customer satisfaction'.

Equally, if the business wishes to be operational excellent, then perhaps the sales team needs to change the kind of orders it chases, the previous targets having been the result of a C.I.-orientated performance measure.

Of course, it is unlikely that a supplier can actually effect such changes in the customer, but its understanding of the situation, its awareness of the political manifestation of such issues, and its calm advice on possible solutions will go a long way to securing you that coveted strategic supplier status.

A manufacturer of pigments to a bathroom sealants manufacturer observes an internal battle going on between Sales and Production. The sales force (C.I. driven) are pressing for an ever wider range of colours (good news for the pigment supplier) to satisfy consumer and retailer demands, but most of the new colours proposed will only ever be sold in small quantities and the impact on the plant (O.E. driven) of so many small-scale batches will be wholly negative.

The plant continually rejects the demands and it looks as if sales force and supplier will both be disappointed. So the supplier goes into value machine mode and brings in some of its own production people with a suggestion. The plant can make two 'big batches', one of white and one of 'plain', which is in fact a reduction on the current number of lines, so a good thing for their operational excellence. The white batch is taken through to completion of the process while a final application is made to the 'plain' batch just before completion – the addition of different pigments to achieve the variety of colour lines required.

The supplier, by understanding the ambitions the clashes _and_ the potential solution, was the hero, and its reward was twofold: a substantial increase in business on high-margin pigments, and the recognition as an expert in matters of production – a strategic supplier indeed.

What is their money-making logic?

There is no simpler question than 'do we help them make money?' and you would expect any supplier to know the answer without much thought, and yet it often seems to fox them, particularly if you add: 'and how much?'. It is as Alvin Toffler once said: 'Profits, like sausages, are esteemed most by those who know least about what goes into them'.

One reason for this surprising lack of understanding often lies at the door of the buyer, who may be inclined to suggest various different money-making logics if doing so will gain them some advantage over the seller. That such subterfuge does not ultimately help the customer is something that has frustrated sales professionals for as long as there have been sales professionals, but such is life when the customer is in pursuit of a short-term gain.

There are so many choices (Figure 8.10 suggests just some of the options facing a business aiming to improve its profitability) that there is as much scope for disagreement within a company, particularly between functions, as there is over value drivers or the source of competitive advantage (see above). For the supplier wanting 'the truth' the best advice has to be: try to understand the principles behind the customer's business processes, aim for the broadest range of contact points in order to facilitate that understanding, and keep up a constant debate within your own team based on what you see and hear.

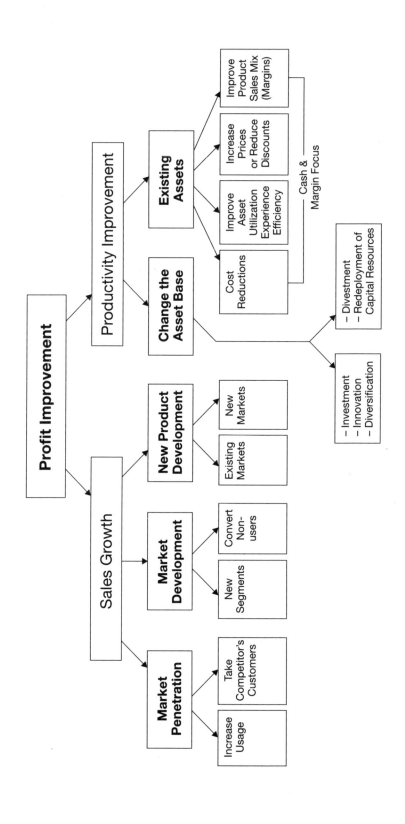

Figure 8.10 *Some options for improving profitability*

The retail industry displays a fine range of money-making logics, from 'pile it high and sell it cheap' to the specialist aiming for high margins based on range and service, and there are plenty of exotic 'logics' in between.

I once sold to a cash-and-carry chain that I confess had me worried and confused. On inspecting their selling prices I found that they were selling my products at zero margins, which meant that, considering their costs of handling, they were losing money on every sale. It wasn't a case of loss leading, these were non-promoted lines hidden away in the corners of the warehouse, so was it a mistake? I made enquiries and found the prices to be as the customer intended.

Convinced that this was no way to build my business with them I set on a plan to extend their ranges, adding items that could sell for proper margins. I was surprised to find them resistant, with always the same response – we only want to stock your fastest movers.

For the best part of six months I persuaded, cajoled, badgered, nagged and bullied, but all to no avail. I even suggested a sale-or-return trial, but that too was rejected. Worse, I could tell that I was starting to irritate them...

Finally they took me aside and gave me a little education. I was reminded that they had negotiated particularly long payment terms – 90 days instead of the normal 30 – and that as a cash-and-carry they offered no form of credit to their customers. If they focused on the fastest-selling lines in any range then the number of times they could turn the stock before the invoice arrived was the secret to a very nice cash generator. That cash was then put to other, more remunerative uses, in other retail outlets owned by the same parent – a simple enough money-making logic but one that had passed me by.

From that point on our joint business boomed – I focused on the fast movers, and made whatever suggestions I could to get them moving yet faster. So why had they not told me in the first place? That was the final piece of my education: 'suppliers who think we are suffering are often more generous with their terms' they said. Welcome to the real world.

What are they like?

We began this section on achieving strategic supplier status through an understanding of the customer's business strategy with four questions:

1. How do they plan to grow?
2. How do they plan to compete?
3. What makes them excel?
4. What is their money-making logic?

These are important questions that allow us to explore deep into the workings of the customer, but some might think them a little cold, even sterile, so we will end the section with one last and rather more 'people orientated' question: what are they like?

As well as matching with the customer's purchasing and business strategies, we also need to think about matching on a more human level: matching their behaviours, or what we might call their business and operational culture. For some people this part of the matching process is the icing on the cake, while for others it is the route to the cake itself.

Business culture is the result of many strands, and it is not the place of this book to begin a lengthy discussion of any of those strands in particular, rather, to give a list of the kind of areas in which you might need to observe the customer's attitudes and behaviours. Once observed, you can begin to determine the likelihood of a match under present circumstances, or the need for, or desirability of, any modifications to your own behaviours.

When I say 'your own behaviours' I refer of course to the whole supplier team, so the idea of modifying behaviours is a significant one. No more than with the business strategy this is not necessarily about becoming the same as the customer, but ensuring that you are relevant. Sometimes that will require direct mirroring, sometimes it may be better to stand out from the crowd – the advantage of going through this process of analysis is simply that you know the options and the possibilities.

It may be that as you get closer to a customer you realize that their culture is *very* different to yours, and in important areas; perhaps they have a rather different interpretation of business ethics to yours, and at this point alarm bells should be ringing. It is one thing to adapt your own organization in order to match business needs, but should you go as far as adapting your stand on ethical issues? Only you can decide. For myself, I would be asking at such a point whether it is necessary to review just how far we wish this particular relationship to develop.

Nobody should be asked to 'play-act' in front of a customer; this is dangerous territory and at some point you tend to get found out. So, the following list is a suggestion of the kinds of area that you might need to examine (with some inevitably vague definitions of a spectrum in each case) with three ends in mind: first, to understand the customer's culture, then to assess the likelihood of a match as things stand, and finally to determine what steps, if any, might be taken to enhance the matching process. Some areas are easier than others, and how far you go will be entirely down to your own circumstances, capabilities and ambitions. There is no golden rule, other than to observe and to understand – once that is done, the necessary actions become so much clearer.

- dress code: informal – formal – uniform;
- entertainment: none – internal only – supplier provided;
- meeting venues: the customer's – neutral – the supplier's;
- meeting style: 1:1 – ad hoc – teams;
- organizational structure: hierarchies – teams – flat;
- management control: open – federal – centralized;
- management style: empowered – process led – individualistic;
- internal communications: informal – ad hoc – formal;
- career development: ad hoc – fluid – structured;
- time horizons: short – medium – long;
- attitude to risk: averse – shared with suppliers – entrepreneurial;
- growth aspirations: low – medium – high;
- growth methodology: organic – mixed – acquisition;
- ethics: weak – pragmatic – strong.

NEW TASK, NEW LANGUAGE – REPLACING THE 4 P'S

Back in the opening chapter I said that the development of a value machine organization and approach would require the rethinking of many 'long cherished' conventions, not to say anachronisms. One in particular was mentioned – the 4 P's of marketing. This is the model that divides the supplier's marketing task into four neat compartments: the product, the promotion, the place, and the price. That it works cannot be denied, it remains the foundation of perhaps most marketing operations, but we need to question its appropriateness in a true value machine outlook.

The problem with the 4 P's is that they all involve _doing things to_ the market and the customers within that market, and what we seek in the value machine is strategic collaboration through a matching process. This calls for a rather more subtle relationship. Rather than throw the baby out with the bathwater, we might retain the idea of four activities, but reframe them with new words – words that indicate a more collaborative approach.

In place of the _'product'_ – which in the old model is about just that, _our_ product – I might suggest the _'solution'_ – meaning: what combination of products, services and relationships is required to develop the customer's business along the lines they wish while enhancing our own rewards from the process? The product remains, but it is only one part of this new equation.

In place of _'promotion'_ – which in the old model is about us throwing messages at the customer – how about a _'conversation'_ – meaning: how do we plan to keep each other informed about the important elements of our business and our capabilities?

In place of the *'price'* – which as we know is no more than a marker to be haggled over – I might suggest the *'value'* – meaning: what is the true worth of our proposition to the customer, measured in their own terms, and how does that determine the nature of our reward?

In place of *'place'* (always the clumsiest of the four P's) – which in the old model is about our choice of channels to market and the means of working through them – I suggest *'collaboration'* – meaning: how do we plan to act in concert with our customers in order to get our joint solutions to the market? So, no handy acronym I'm afraid, but something more important than that, the start of a new set of collaborative attitudes and behaviours expressed through new language.

If all of this seems pure semantics to you then I apologize. I rather hope that it is more than that, perhaps a trigger to start you thinking about how to change the attitudes and thought processes within your own organization. In that pursuit of course you must use whatever language suits best, and if the old four P's can still be made to work under the old names but with new definitions relevant to the principles of the value machine then that is just fine.

Sometimes the management of change requires the use of symbols to act as signposts, and the use of new language can often be a powerful, though uncomfortable, part of that symbolic process. Think of the huge progress made in the last 20 years in regard to what is said in public (and thought in private) about differences of gender, race, religion and ethnicity. *Political correctness* has always been easy to knock, but through its processes we have changed the language we use, and so in time the thoughts that we think. The same can be true for those wanting to change the thoughts and behaviours that go to make up a business culture.

The value machine's matching process and the hoped-for collaborative working that follows will almost certainly call for a new vocabulary, and the politically wise (not to say 'correct') supplier could do worse than adopting the customer's.

9

The value creation process

The culmination of the matching process must be the creation of an enhanced value proposition. If it isn't this, then what was the point of all that effort? The *enhancement* is on both sides of the collaborative process of course – more appropriate and impactful value for the customer, and a better reward for the supplier, from the customer and from within their own organization.

All those efforts to build deep and broad relationships, to understand the customer's market and their business, to identify and match their strategies, their values and their drivers, all of this brings us to this point: the creation of value.

We might begin with a few observations (mostly reminders) on the nature of value propositions, or at least, value propositions of the value machine kind:

- Value is *received* by the customer, into their business processes, in a way that is relevant to their business needs, ambitions or strategy.
- Value impacts at those points in the customer's *total business experience* (see below), where problems exist and solutions can be found.
- Value is created through a *collaborative partnership* between customer and supplier; developing and matching the supplier's capabilities to the true needs of the customer.
- Value improves over time; enhanced through the fine tuning of experience and continued collaboration.
- The supplier's rewards improve over time, through *enhanced capabilities*.

THE CUSTOMER'S TOTAL BUSINESS EXPERIENCE (TBE)

If we remember that customers *receive* value, then we can see how that value is part of their business experience – their experience of dealing with the supplier, their experience of performing their own operations, and their experience of dealing with their own customers. We might call the sum of that trio their *total business experience* (TBE).

The well-matched strategic supplier will have their finger on the pulse of that experience – cradle to grave – and in particular they will know where it goes wrong. Problems are at the heart of true value propositions – no problem, no solution, no value.

> On a recent long-haul flight I was intrigued by a new entertainment system promising to let me watch up to 80 movies *simultaneously*. What this meant was that I could watch 10 minutes of a movie, freeze it, watch 5 minutes of a second, freeze that, go back to the first for a further 5 minutes, freeze it again, open a third and watch 15 minutes (obviously a good one...), and so on up to 80. Absolutely brilliant, that is as far as the technology was concerned – but why; what was the problem? Actually it gave me a new problem – how to work the system (I spent the best part of half an hour struggling with the instructions...).
>
> Now I know what you are thinking – what an old fuddy-duddy – if I had been a 12-year-old kid then just think of how much time I could burn. Fine, I agree, but I must say that I don't meet too many 12-year-old kids travelling long-haul business class...
>
> Here was an example, at least from *this* customer's perspective, of a value proposition gone wrong – great idea, but no problem, so no solution required and no value received (other than a story to tell...).

This case, and many more like it, represent not only the problems of a value proposition 'gone wrong' in front of the customer but also the great deal of wasted effort within the supplier's own organization. Such things happen when suppliers focus on their own products and benefits; like staring at individual trees while failing to see the forest of the customer's real needs. Sometimes this product focus can result in complete inaction even when the customer's needs are staring you in the face.

> Food retailers back in the 1980s were always complaining about the receipt of damaged goods from suppliers of fruit and vegetables. In response the suppliers would argue that the customers' demands for ready-to-eat freshness almost

mandated a certain amount of damage. The suppliers concentrated on the freshness issue – they had put a lot of effort into it over the years – and the complaints went on.

No surprise that the retailers at last took the problem into their own hands, going above the heads of their suppliers, and approaching a supplier of plastic crates. They insisted that their fresh-produce suppliers should purchase and use these crates in the delivery of their products, reducing damage dramatically, and also ensuring a uniform method of supply at their backdoors.

This solution – a value proposition if there ever was one – was imposed on suppliers by a customer frustrated by those suppliers' complete inability to understand their TBE. No surprise then that the solution was entirely a cost to the suppliers with no prospect of being rewarded for their newly enhanced performance.

So, is it a race to the solution? If the customer gets there first then there will be slim reward for the supplier. If the supplier gets there first then… but how can they, without the collaboration of the customer? It is as we said earlier in the chapter: value is created through a *collaborative partnership* between customer and supplier, developing and matching the supplier's capabilities to the true needs of the customer.

In truth, someone usually needs to take the lead, and why not the supplier? A good supplier should take more interest in a customer's problems than the customer themselves – for the customer, a problem is merely something to be solved, for the supplier, a problem is their lifeblood. For a supplier to deliver genuine value and, as importantly, be rewarded for it, they have to understand the nature of the customer's problems better than the customer themselves. The good news is that is sufficient to be just one step ahead.

THE CUSTOMER'S ACTIVITY CYCLE

This is the tool that allows us to keep that one step ahead, illustrated in Figure 9.1, and it is one of the simplest in the toolkit, yet also one of the most effective in bringing to life the matching process of the value machine.

The tool maps out around a circle all of the customer's activities: in doing business with their supplier, in their own internal processes, and in dealing with their own customers. These three stages of their *total business experience* equate roughly to the 'before, during and after' stages shown in Figure 9.1.

As much detail as possible should be noted and included; it is often among the minutia of business transactions that the gems of true value are to be

Figure 9.1 *The customer's activity cycle*

found. A team is essential for this task of course, the cross-functional supplier team bringing its range of perspectives and experiences. Suppliers that bemoan their lack of customer knowledge are almost always pleasantly surprised when they start to pool the 'corporate knowledge' of their own team. One golden rule – this is the customer's activity cycle, not the supplier's. We are not logging what the supplier does, but what the customer does, and that will usually call for some extra research. Doubtless the supplier already has a good idea of what goes on, but through the efforts of a properly briefed cross-functional team the additional detail will start to flow. Don't be afraid of question marks – if you don't know what the customer does next then this is simply a trigger to your next piece of research.

Many people will say that they have no interaction with the customer in the 'after' portion of this cycle – the customer's activities with their own customers. Think more broadly: if you have supplied a raw material, then you are intimately involved in the customer's 'after' – your product is inside their product, and is either contributing to that product's success, or is instrumental in its failure...

Suppliers with a limited knowledge of the customer's activity cycle run the risk of making only a limited impact. Everyone knows how the customer places their order and receives the product, but if that is all you know, as illustrated in Figure 9.2, then the search for 'solutions' is going to be rather limited.

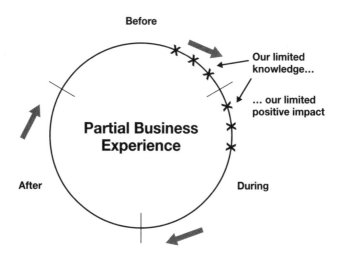

Figure 9.2 _Limited knowledge – limited positive impact_

The key is of course in the problems – where does it go wrong in the customer's experience? – and by extending our knowledge of the customer's activities the likelihood of finding additional problems is inevitably increased. Figure 9.3 shows a completed cycle with the customer's problems identified.

Figure 9.3 _The problems in the customer's activity cycle_

This is where we focus our attentions; bringing in the appropriate expertise from our own team, matching them with the appropriate contacts on the customer's side, developing a collaborative approach to the solution, and most importantly, being seen to take the lead in all of this – that vital one step ahead.

Of course, some of these problems might be out of our scope to address, or at least out of our *current* scope. One of the beauties of this tool can be its role in spurring our ambitions, but I am perhaps getting a little ahead of myself. The key to making this tool work is to take it in stages. Resist the temptation to leap at 'bright ideas' before you have properly mapped out the full cycle, step by step, detail by detail, ploddingly and meticulously.

There is a proper order in which to tackle this exercise, proceeding through three distinct phases:

1. the activity analysis;
2. the problem/solution analysis;
3. the positive impact analysis.

The activity analysis

1. Identify the specific customer circumstance – what products and services does this involve? – and identify the supplier team required to work on the analysis.
2. What is the customer's overall ambition – the aim of their total business experience?
3. Map out the customer's activities, in as much detail as possible.
4. Identify the gaps in your knowledge and take steps to fill them – research, questions, involving others in your own team.

The problem/solution analysis

1. Identify those points in the cycle where the customer experiences problems.
2. Do you already make attempts to impact on those problems?:
   - How successfully?
   - What value do you add?
   - Do you get an appropriate reward?
3. How do your competitors stand on these – do they do a better or worse job than you?
4. What solutions could be developed to make an enhanced impact on those problems?

Step 4 is of course the biggest and toughest of the steps and not something to be attempted or concluded in an hour around a flipchart. You will almost certainly want several visits on this, interspersed with further research. You will certainly need to bring in additional people – colleagues from those functions most able to make an impact, and perhaps people from outside the business but with similar or analogous experiences.

Don't attempt this on your own, or as a single function – it has already been noted that this is an exercise crying out for a cross-functional team approach from the very outset.

Perhaps you might even seek the help of the customer, or if we wish to be true to the principles of the value machine we had better ask: _when_ do we bring in the customer's team?

The customer's involvement has to be the ideal scenario from three viewpoints: detailed knowledge, the development of closer relationships, and ability to implement through a collaborative partnership.

But take care not to rush their involvement. For one thing, they may be suspicious of your motives in taking such a close interest in their minutiae. For another, you will want to get your own act together first. It is best to involve the customer once you already have a good idea of what goes on – you can look very foolish for not knowing what they may take to be something obvious in the 'what happens next' process.

Finally, a health warning. This exercise can be a very fertile source of new ideas, of new things 'to do', and you almost certainly do not intend doing them all. You will be selective, screening the ideas for the best – meaning the best for both customer and supplier. Without care you can easily leave the customer with the impression that you are about to do everything that was discussed, and that way leads to huge disappointment on their part and the destruction of all your good work. Manage their expectations from the outset. Make clear the purpose of the exercise, perhaps agree the criteria for final screening and selection, or perhaps agree that you are only looking for one new action at a time – however you do it, avoid the sin of building their expectations only to have them come crashing down.

The positive impact analysis

On completing the second phase of the exercise we have arrived at a range of possible solutions. Each one of these represents an investment, each with its own potential return. It is almost inevitable that there will be ideas that can be implemented quickly and easily but that offer only small returns, and those that will require huge effort but promise similar returns (if ever there are simple to implement but big return ideas, jump on those quickly!). So which to choose?

145

No supplier is likely to be able to work on all of the ideas at once, and nor would they wish to even if they could. There is little point in bringing six great ideas to the customer all at once. For a start they are more likely to be confused than delighted, and even if they are delighted they will soon forget your brilliance and be looking for the next good idea – and you have blown them all at once! There is a better plan.

Suppose you were an athlete, a pole-vaulter let's say, and have discovered in training that you can beat the world record height by a full metre. You might rush to the next international Grand Prix meeting and stun the world with your incredible prowess, or you might just beat the record by a centimetre and go away happy. Why might you do the latter? Because you will have been awarded a good deal of money for your achievement and at the very next Grand Prix meeting you will do it again, and for the same large amount of money. If your career lasts long enough you might even manage to repeat your achievement another 98 times. That's the way to get rich and famous.

If you have six great ideas, spread them out over a period of time. Win yourself a reputation as a supplier that always has another new trick up its sleeve – a supplier worth working with. That's the way to get respected, and rich...

We still have the question however: *which* great idea first? We need to screen the 'possibles', selecting those that represent the best investments. We will call this part of the exercise the *positive impact analysis* (PIA).

Our task is complicated by the fact that we are making two separate but related comparisons: what promises to make the most positive impact on the customer, and what promises to give the best return for ourselves? A standard directional policy matrix (DPM) might fit the bill, a four-box matrix as shown in Figure 9.4.

Figure 9.4 *Investment appraisal*

On the horizontal axis we might ask the following kinds of question, to determine the attractiveness of the project to the customer (you will recognize many of them from our assessment of their business strategy in Chapter 8):

● Does it reduce or remove a known problem?
● How urgent is the problem so removed/reduced?
● Does it help them to grow as they plan?
● Does it help them to reduce risk?
● Does it help renew or extend their product lifecycle?
● Does it give them competitive advantage?
● Does it impact positively on their core value drivers?
● Does it contribute to their money-making logic?
● Does this bring them savings in time or money – cost reductions, faster processes, etc?
● Does it resonate with the customer?
● Is it of high value (using the customer's definition of value received)?

To properly answer this last question it will be necessary to quantify the value received in each of the preceding questions – not always easy and not always possible, but this is not an exact science – at some point we must exercise our judgement.

On the vertical axis we might ask a carefully chosen selection from the following kinds of question, to determine the attractiveness of the project to ourselves:

● Will the rewards (price, revenue, volume, share, access, etc) outweigh the costs? (I leave the niceties of things such as _comparative discounted cash flows_ to your own experts.)
● Do we have the capability?
● Can we develop the capability, and at a cost that still gives us an acceptable return?
● Does it give us sustainable competitive advantage (and for how long)?
● Does it give us 'lock in' (see below)?
● Will the customer grant us some premium reward (price, volume, share, access, other projects, etc)?
● Does it help us to avoid competitive disadvantage (will it prevent a competitor stealing a march on us)?
● Does it improve our own efficiency (economies of scale, improved processes, etc) or effectiveness (enhanced capabilities, etc)?
● Does it allow us to enhance our value propositions to other customers or markets?

This assessment does not automatically assume that we go for those in the top right-hand box (the win–win options if you like). We should ask, and as honestly as we can: is it possible to increase the attractiveness of something to the customer that lies in the top-left box? If we can, through our skills of persuasion, then this is clearly good news for us, but take care not to fool yourself – honesty is key.

We should also ask, and again with great honesty: are those ideas that fall into the bottom-right box *really* so unattractive to us? If they are so attractive to the customer cannot that, by those same good persuasion skills, be turned to our advantage? This is not about talking yourself into something that is in truth not good for you – simply a double check.

Even now, having shifted some ideas around in the matrix, we still don't automatically aim for those in the top right because there is one last question to ask: what impression are we trying to make?

Let's say we are dealing with a Key Development Account and you need to impress them reasonably quickly in order to gain further access. You might choose one of the lower return investments simply because it is easier to complete at speed. You might even deliberately choose one that favours the customer more than it favours you – as a part of the 'courting' process. Or perhaps this is a Key Account with which you have been working for some time on a number of small issues of no great consequence. Perhaps it is now time to go for the 'big one' even though it has a timetable of three years to completion? This has to be one to be decided through discussion and judgement; there are no more four-box matrices to help us here!

LOCK-IN AND COLLABORATION

One of the criteria used for judging the attractiveness of an idea to the supplier was: does it give us *lock-in*? Lock-in is the concept that we can bind the customer more closely to us through our offer, perhaps even exclusively, so making it harder for our competition to operate. An example might be the use of telemetry in providing an automatic reordering system for a liquid held in a customer's silo. A gauge in the silo registers the reorder point and everything is set in motion. For the competitor to get involved the automatic system has to be turned off and the customer has to place a manual order. This might just be too much effort for them to consider unless the competitor's price is significantly lower, and if it isn't, the original supplier has achieved lock-in.

So lock in is considered a 'good thing', for the supplier, but here we hit on a potential problem. Lock-in can be seen as rather threatening from the customer's perspective. Lock-in inevitably increases the significance of the supplier and so the level of risk borne by the customer and also their level of dependency. This may even run counter to their purchasing strategy where they might be attempting to reduce their exposure to overly significant suppliers (as described in Chapter 8 – the Kraljic Matrix – see Figure 8.6 and the opposing arrow directions).

So, is lock-in a good or a bad idea in the realm of collaborative partnerships?

The issue is largely one of power, and that is always a delicate balance. Lock in increases supplier power, and so suppliers must tread carefully. The airline that offers to manage its corporate clients full business travel arrangements must take great care not to abuse its position – flying their client from London to Moscow via New York (the airline has no direct flight) is not value, it is an outrage!

> One of the most famous examples of a misplaced attempt at lock-in was that of Apple. Apple had a truly splendid operating system but they wanted to hang on to it and to use its strength to sell their own machines; you could only have it if you bought an Apple computer. This effectively restricted the value that consumers could receive and when Microsoft allowed MS-Dos to be put on any machine you liked, they won the day. This was effectively an attempt at lock in that got them locked out.

Lock-in will be unpopular if it is used for too obviously selfish ends. Much of the complaint against the development of genetically modified seeds is that they are designed to work only in combination with the seed supplier's own herbicides and pesticides. The notorious 'terminator gene' that would prevent the crop from producing new seed was a step too far, particularly when considering the sale to Third World countries, and that particular attempt at lock in was withdrawn.

As part of a genuine collaboration it can be a great strategy. Let's suppose that the customer wishes their supplier to provide a new product that will be of particular value to them but will require a significant investment in new capability on the part of the supplier. Unfortunately it is not a big-volume item and so there is a natural reluctance from the supplier. There is however the possibility, as the supplier well realizes, to attach a service to the product that would result in lock-in between supplier and customer. The proposition is made to provide the linked product and service and the customer accepts. They are fully aware of the advantage that they are giving the supplier over the competition, a privileged position in fact, but realize that this is precisely the reward required for the supplier to make the appropriate investment. They settle on a win–win outcome, the secret of which was not trickery or cunning sales technique but plain simple mutual benefit.

THE ACTIVITY CYCLE IN ACTION

You are flying the Atlantic on business – what might be your problems? Wasting hours getting through the complexity of airport car parks and shuttle buses? Hanging around in an airport environment where it is impossible to work? Not enough space to work on the plane? A flat PC battery after only two hours on the plane? Eight hours without e-mail? Arriving too tired to do a good job?

Airlines have analysed the activity cycles of such passengers and the result has been a range of services from home pick-ups to business lounges, from on-board seating plans with workspace and hook-ups for laptops to pyjamas and eiderdowns.

But what if you are travelling on holiday; is any of that stuff of interest to you? Probably not, and the airline will conduct another activity cycle to identify the right package for such travellers. A particular favourite of mine is the facility provided by Virgin Atlantic to check in for your return flight from Orlando, Florida inside the Disney Parks. The problem identified was the last day of the holiday, which was not part of the holiday at all. Now you can have another day with Mickey Mouse, an extra day's holiday, free.

And what if your real issue is that you are a diabetic, and long-haul flights are a major problem for taking your insulin? Insulin needs to be taken at particular times, often relative to when you eat, but airlines make you eat when they want you to eat... Not on some airlines; those that allow you to choose the time of your meal, and so secure the loyalty of such passengers.

The ferries from Eire to the UK see a lot of racehorse traffic, and in the past a lot of worried-looking stable lads. Consider their problem. They're responsible for several million pounds' worth of horse and they have to leave it down in the hold while they fret upstairs, worrying about what it might be doing to itself.

The solution, identified after a careful analysis of what such travellers went through on their trips, was the provision of a video camera to put in the horsebox, linked to viewers in specially equipped lounges for the stable lads.

Suppliers to the retail industry talk of 'category management'; the idea that they should base their propositions on a combination of the retailer's and the consumer's perceptions of value received, all of which is considered against the broader canvas of the market segment, not simply the supplier's own product. A good category manager is interested in the total health of the category, not just any one product within that category. The activity cycle is a great way to understand these issues.

A food supplier such as Kraft combines their knowledge of the consumer (after) with their knowledge of the retailer (before and during) to deliver a high-value proposition to both. In the United States, Kraft has segmented their consumers into six broad types based on their shopping behaviour. They have then designed specific ranges of products to appeal to these six types in different ways. Working with the retailer, they assess what balance of these six types shop in each of the retailer's stores, and plan the store's range and layout accordingly. By looking beyond their immediate customer (the retailer), Kraft is able to add value to that customer, and to the final consumer offer.

THE APPROPRIATE REWARD

It is when we use a tool like the customer activity cycle, in collaboration with the customer, that we see again how the relationship itself has value. It is through working together that we open up the possibilities for value through our products and services – and the relationship came first. The relationship is an investment every bit as much as any R&D project or new logistics system, and is every bit as deserving of an appropriate reward.

In the context of a simple transactional sale the supplier's reward is usually measured in some combination of price and volume. In the context of the value machine the reward takes on more ambitious proportions, to include things such as enhanced supplier capabilities, the greater effectiveness of internal resources, the development of an enhanced value proposition to this and other customers, longer term sustainability, and plenty more besides. Much of this reward doesn't need to be secured from the customer, it comes from within the supplier's own organization and is not subject to the wiles of a professional purchaser across the negotiating table. So much is good news, except that the customer may just be aware of that, and may seek to argue a discount for all the benefits that they have helped you to find!

Once upon a time oil companies just supplied oil, but as their processes became more sophisticated, and as their involvement on the customer's site deepened, so some of them found that they had developed a new and broader expertise: managing fluid supplies on a customer's site. For their most important customers

> BP will offer to manage the customer's 'total fluid requirements'. This will almost certainly involve taking responsibility for the supply of products outside their own portfolio, perhaps in some cases even working with a competitor's products. The focus moves to reducing the volumes of product required and improving efficiencies of use – providing lower costs rather than lowest prices. Indeed, the price of the product itself becomes of less and less relevance as the broader services are charged for in more creative, more holistic ways.

The secret to getting the right reward for a value proposition is not to be found at the negotiating table, it is to be found in knowledge – knowing who receives your value, what they can do with it, and so what it is worth. Knowing what it is worth requires us to know how to measure the value received, and in the customer's terms. Unfortunately most customers don't tell you such things. For a start it isn't the way they are trained to go about a supplier negotiation, but for another, they probably haven't got around to measuring themselves. This should be no problem to any supplier worthy of the value machine mantle – such a supplier should be perfectly able to do the sums on the customer's behalf.

Start by using the right language. For a start, don't measure things using your own terminology – use theirs.

> It is not so very long ago that a conversation between a brewery and one of its retail customers might have proceeded as follows:
>
> 'Good news, last month you purchased 5,000 more barrels of our beer than in the same month last year.'
>
> 'No, we didn't,' would come the reply from the customer.
>
> 'I'm sorry, perhaps I should have showed you my sales statistics – look, 5,000 barrels more.'
>
> But once again came the same reply: 'No, we didn't'.
>
> 'I'm sorry, I don't understand.'
>
> 'Well, I don't recall a single one of your barrels coming into a single one of our stores. We bought cans, and bottles, and four-packs, but no barrels. That's how you brewers measure your volume, or hectolitres or some such... '
>
> The lesson was learned quickly enough, at least by the sales people, but it was still a while before head office was prepared to change the way they reported sales: 'how can we compare off trade to on trade if we use different measures?' they said.
>
> There was a more important question: 'How can we measure customer value if we don't even use their units of volume?'

Wherever possible value should be expressed by the customer's outputs, not by the supplier inputs. It's a harder task of course, and one that requires a significant understanding of the customer's circumstances, but this is precisely what we have been aiming for with the use of the activity cycle tool.

Figure 9.5 illustrates a successful approach, where customers have been helped to measure value by their own outputs. It also explains why 'model C' dominates the heavy-user segment of the office printer market.

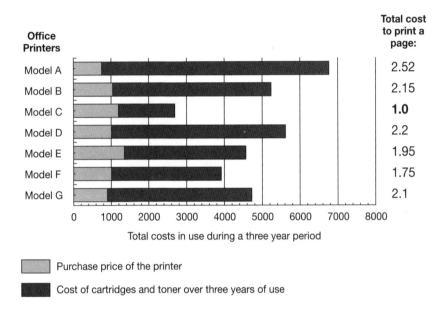

Figure 9.5 _Measuring the value of an office printer_

Model C is the second most expensive to buy, but its superior efficiency in using toner gives it an excellent 'cost in use' proposition; important if you are a heavy user. But the real secret to its success is the way that it has helped its customers to recognize that value.

Model C doesn't talk about its selling price much, nor even the reduced cost in use that results from its efficient toner use, it has a far simpler message; the cost to the customer of printing a page of paper.

Now I confess that this is a fairly simple task for the supplier in this case – all the measurements are easy to hand. The task for a supplier of a material or service used in the manufacture of another product is a much tougher one, but worth the effort nonetheless.

The aim should be for some basis of measurement that matches up to the following criteria:

- it is measurable and quantifiable;
- it can be presented using the customer's terms;
- it matters to the customer;
- it will give you a sustainable competitive advantage;
- it will allow you to secure an appropriate reward.

THE VALUE MACHINE BRAND

There is another kind of matching that we might consider: that of the supplier's brand with the customer's aspirations. Brands can be explained in many ways – each new book on the subject suggests a new analogy – but within the context of the value machine there is a very particular definition.

The sign of a good brand is that it occupies a relevant space in the target customer's mind, cementing itself there through a series of relevant interactions. In other words, the good brand is a successful match between the customer's aspirations and the supplier's recognized capabilities.

Positioning the brand

First, the brand has to be 'positioned', and with precision. An *under positioned* brand is one that stands for nothing in particular, occupies no particular space in the customer's mind, and gives the customer little reason to buy, or even to care. An *over positioned* brand has become too specific, focused on too narrowly defined a group of customers, and once they've bought, it's done. A *confusingly positioned* brand is one trying to be too many things at once – contradictions and conflicts abound in the customer's mind. An *irrelevantly positioned* brand has a value proposition about which nobody cares. A *doubtfully positioned* brand is one that makes claims that nobody believes, taking it beyond the realm of the supplier's recognized capabilities.

Brands don't always get it right the first time around…

> Marlboro, one of the earliest filter-tip cigarettes, was originally positioned to appeal to women, and failing to make great headway there it tried to target men where its filter tip was considered positively 'sissy'. Finally they adopted a cowboy for an image and repositioned the brand as the 'he-man's smoke'. The rest is history.

Getting it right with your target customers, and with precision, almost inevitably means a measure of misunderstanding or even disapproval by those not targeted – the 'what's that all about then?' syndrome. Universally acclaimed brands are rare, and dangerous examples to copy. 'Disapproved of' brands can be surprisingly successful. Some measure of disapproval is almost essential when a new brand tries to break into a mature market.

> Häagen Dazs was launched in an environment that supposed ice cream was for kids; they needed to create a new space in people's minds, escaping from those associations. The brand was shown with adult interactions, sometimes with provocative images that could only bring disapproval from some, but helped establish a loyalty from those specifically targeted.

Some brands even manage to play cleverly on their realization that not everyone likes them. Marmite sought to position its unique taste by recognizing that some folk just can't stand the stuff –'I hate' Marmite posters ran alongside the 'My Mate' posters in one hugely successful advertising campaign.

Some brand managers might use the idea of personalities (types, or even specific individuals) to help describe their positioning. This can be a useful concept when wanting to change the brand's position. Think about how a person might go about changing their personality? They might change their clothes, their hairstyle, their accent, their behaviour, but the problem is that their family and friends still remember who they were before all this confusing messing about. If a person really wants to change their personality they often find that they just have to leave home. Repositioning a brand often involves much the same process.

> Time was when Lucozade was what your mother bought for you when you were ill. Generations grew up identifying the brand with illness and recuperation. It was a clear positioning but one with limited potential for growth. SmithKline Beecham, the brand's owner, conducted a brilliant campaign over a number of years to reposition the product as a high-energy 'sports drink'. SB had identified the potential in this segment and they had a product with many of the necessary attributes. High-profile product endorsements from the likes of Daley Thompson were used to great effect alongside new packaging designs and new target retail outlets. Lucozade is still a favourite choice for those overcoming illness, but it now also occupies a position well away from the invalid's bedside table.

Predictor, a self-use pregnancy testing kit, found that its personality was not entirely suited to its growth aspirations. The product was well thought of, reliable and responsible, but it suffered from some negative associated images – unpleasant surprises, let-downs, unwanted pregnancies. It was too often a product that you bought when trouble was looming. While that might have been a base on which to position the brand – a promise of performance in use – it wasn't where Predictor wanted to be. They wanted the brand to have a more upbeat emotional charge, and so a more prominent place in the customer's mind: personal fulfilment. A combination of a packaging redesign and an advertising campaign demonstrating the joy, private and public, of discovering your dreams come true helped to put the brand on to this new level.

The positioning process

Figure 9.6 illustrates the three-step positioning process.

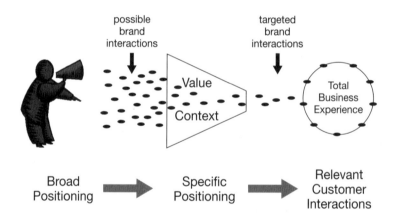

Figure 9.6 *Brand positioning – the process*

Step 1 is an assessment of the general supplier or product capabilities that *could* be communicated through the brand to the target market/ segment/customer. Sometimes referred to as the brand's *broad positioning* we should note carefully the use of the word 'could'. Brands usually need a finer focus than a broad list of everything they can do. Many B2B brands suffer from this 'list' syndrome, becoming not so much brands as catalogues.

Step 2 is that all-important focus, taking the list of capabilities and translating it into a *specific positioning*; which particular capabilities do you want the customer to recognize? There are many methodologies used for finding that focus; we will look at three: the _benefits_ approach, the _value context_ approach (illustrated in Figure 9.6), and the _emotional charge_ approach. They will be seen to overlap each other, taking slightly different perspectives on the issue, but they all have one thing in common: the desire to match with what the customer expects to get from the brand.

Specific benefits…

It is quite common for a B2B brand to take the benefits of its value proposition and use that as its focus. This is fine if the proposition is already well developed and if the benefits are specific and simple enough to communicate through the brand definition, and if they are of common interest to the whole target market. Quite a string of 'ifs', but it can be done.

Volvo has for many years defined its brand through the benefit of safety. 'No FT, no comment' makes it clear the benefit that this newspaper brings its customers. Berri, an Australian fruit juice, has defined itself through the benefit of patriotism – it is '100 per cent Australian owned'. Many a malt whisky brand has taken heritage and traditional values as its source benefit. The Hovis brand reassures us with 'as good for you today as its always been' benefit. Some brands even find their source benefit through comparison to the competition – Avis 'tries harder', Duracel 'lasts longer'.

There is always a danger of claiming too much, and so confusing customers with too many benefits. In general, the greater the number of benefits argued the more diffused and diluted the brand definition becomes – the less precise the matching process. While this might allow the brand to work across many segments it will also leave it open to a competitor that that takes a more single-minded approach.

The value context…

The _value context_ is a statement of intent and acts as a funnel, helping us to identify which of our many capabilities we wish to promote through the brand. There are five main choices, and all can work – the trick is to make sure that you remain consistent with your choice.

- Getting more for more – the 'reassuringly expensive' Stella Artois, or premium priced Häagen Dazs.
- Getting more for the same – plenty of 'added value' B2B brands aspire to this slot, obliged to match competitor prices and slugging it out over competing benefits…

- Getting more for less – the so-called *category-killer* retail brands such as Wal*Mart where their scale and buying power promises bigger ranges, greater choice and lower prices.
- Getting the same for less – the Lexus. 'Perhaps for the first time in history that trading a $72,000 car for a $36,000 car could be considered trading up' runs one of their ads, or Tesco and its high profile 'rip-off Britain' campaign to sell Levi's jeans at 'non rip-off prices'.
- Getting less for much less – 'stripped down' brands such as Ryanair or easyJet, the Formule 1 hotel chain, or the Netto supermarket chain. These examples show that the *giving* part of the equation is not always money – it might be the sacrifice of amenities, an acceptance of risk, or a 'managed level of discomfort'.

Two options to avoid: 'getting the same for more', and 'getting less for more'…

The emotional charge

Brands are the sum of their interactions with the customer, and those interactions go to make up a particular relationship, good or bad, significant or trivial. The nature of the relationship can be described by the brand's *emotional charge*.

Some brands pull on our emotional responses more than others, depending on a complex interaction of factors:

- the price paid;
- the frequency of purchase;
- the risk involved in the purchase;
- the risk involved in use;
- the conspicuity of the purchase;
- the importance of consistency;
- the utility of the product or service;
- the tangibility of performance;
- the number of brands competing for attention.

The factors don't work in isolation and nor do they always work in the same direction – just because an item is low priced, regularly purchased and has a utilitarian purpose, that doesn't mean that it can't have a high emotional charge.

Toilet paper is a case in point. The Andrex brand spends a lot, and does so consistently, to build emotional responses that go well beyond these factors. The Andrex puppies exude messages of softness, warmth, care and responsibility (at the same time as helping communicate messages about the length of the roll!) – a subtle blend with a strong appeal.

Figure 9.7 illustrates four types of emotional charge, in rising order of 'strength', used typically with consumer brands, but also applicable to some B2B brands.

- A social expression
  *(you'll love **me**, for loving it...)*

- Satisfaction or fulfilment
  *(**I** love it...)*

- The promise of performance in use
  (it does what I need it to do)

- A guarantee of authenticity
  (it's the genuine article)

the
'rising charge'

Figure 9.7   *The emotional charge*

Some brands can work on more than one level, that being a strength provided it doesn't cause confusion. Kellogg's have made much of their statement 'if it doesn't say Kellogg's on the pack, it isn't Kellogg's inside the pack' – a clear statement of *authenticity*, but there are many consumers who gain genuine *satisfaction* from pouring their favourite breakfast cereal from a reassuringly genuine Kellogg's box (not to mention eating the stuff...).

A mark of authenticity

In the days of the USSR, Borjomi sparkling mineral water from the Caucasus in Georgia was said to be the third best-known brand in the Union; the Volga car and Aeroflot took the top spots. By 1996, after a decade or more of the kind of free enterprise that encouraged the rise of piracy and gangsterism, as much as 90 per cent of what went under the Borjomi label was said to be counterfeit! Then came the advertising campaign, reminding consumers of the distinctive packaging of the real Borjomi ('beware imitations'), and the not insignificant financial crisis of 1998 that killed off many of the poorly financed counterfeiters. By 2000 the claim was that

90 per cent of Borjomi sold was genuine. Who knows for sure whether it was 90 per cent or only 50 per cent, but what was certain from the company's revitalized fortunes was that branding simply as a mark of authenticity could still work.

A promise of performance in use

Promises can be broken. When Coca-Cola launched a new formulation 'New Coke', they had a flop on their hands. There were many reasons, but one was undoubtedly the strength of the original product's emotional charge – many consumers felt a promise had been broken.

The simplest promises are often the best simply because they are so easy to communicate through vivid brand images: Fairy Liquid's famous comparison tests, or the Duracel battery in the Christmas toy that goes on, and on, and on...

More complex promises are possible of course. Lycra manages it on three levels – as a high-performance material for manufacturers, as an important sales aid to those manufacturers, and as a guarantee of comfort to consumers.

Satisfaction – pleasure or fulfilment

A brand can do more than promise satisfaction; it can positively aid it. Think of a bottle of wine. Simply seeing the bottle, if we recognize the name and think well of it, can convince us that the taste will be, and then is, good. Try it for yourself in an open and then a blind test and just see if it isn't true (and if you disagree with me then at least you will have enjoyed the enquiry).

There is plenty of hard evidence that headache sufferers will feel better treated or soothed by taking a brand of analgesic that they have heard of rather than an unknown generic. Placebos masquerading as well-known brands have been shown to be more effective than placebos in plain white boxes.

Can a washing powder be elevated to the level of satisfaction or fulfilment? The folk behind the Persil brand believe so and have for many years advertised the product as something more than just the route to clean clothes. The inference of the message is a clean family, putting the washer into the role of protector and carer. If this doesn't quite put washing on a par with eating chocolate or watching movies, by injecting that element of pride into using the brand it certainly raises it above that of plain drudgery.

A social expression

This is about *conspicuous consumption*, though that doesn't mean it has to be expensive. Such brands help their user to make a statement, which might simply be about fitting in with the crowd.

Hofmeister lager was launched successfully in the UK, targeted at young working-class males, a closed shop where beer is concerned and group conformity is the key. Hofmeister used George the bear, a 'dude', to gain them street credibility, and of course those that don't see the appeal of George just aren't in the target segment.

The four levels of emotional charge illustrated in these examples (authenticity, satisfaction, a promise of performance in use, and social expression) complete just one 'set' of many variants. If they might better suit the world of the consumer brand, then the 'set' shown in Figure 9.8 might be better suited to the world of the B2B brand.

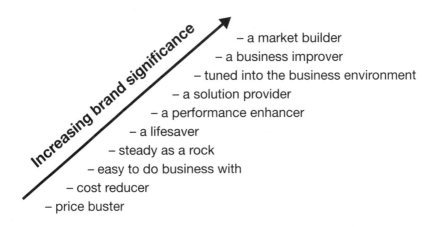

Figure 9.8 *The emotional charge of the B2B brand*

Easy to do business with

American Express takes all the effort out of corporate business travel – that is their claim. The Amex 'in-plant' is a common feature of many a large business, taking on all the tasks short of making the trips themselves. This 'easy to do business with' brand now has to take on the challenge of those managers who think the internet makes it easier for them to do it themselves. The fact that Amex might be better tuned in to their specific business environment may just give them the edge.

161

Steady as a rock

TetraPak is a good example of a brand that is 'steady as a rock'. Its numerous users, often creating new markets made possible by the packaging technology, depend on the absolute reliability of the brand. And if things *do* go wrong, then they depend on the ability of the brand to put them right. TetraPak has much at stake if their product fails the customer, and the customer knows that, and so a strong bond of common interest is forged between supplier, customer, and consumer.

Lifesavers

DHL works hard to define its brand around reliability and speed. Driven by the business world's need to do things fast, and globally, DHL represents a 'life saver' brand. Just hearing the letters DHL brings a sigh of relief – not a bad emotional response to associate with your brand. And then along comes e-mail. Now there is less need for such heroics – huge documents can be sent in seconds with no need for planes, boats and trains. The DHL brand must change into something more than a specialist emergency service. Perhaps a provider of wider business solutions that recognize the changing demands of truly global businesses?

Tuned-in performance enhancers, solution providers, business improvers and market builders

The Intel brand captured the loyalty of PC manufacturers for a variety of reasons, not least because the brand was both a performance enhancer through the ever-increasing speed of their ever-diminishing chips, and a market builder through their consumer franchise. Times change and the PC builders are becoming more interested in cost reduction in a maturing, not to say saturated market. Should Intel take its brand down a price-buster road or should it stick to its market-builder definition by encouraging the development of software applications that will demand its high-speed capabilities? Which would you choose?

And so we get to Step 3 of the positioning process illustrated in Figure 9.6. Having defined our *specific position* we must now create the relevant customer interactions that will bring that positioning to life. The key word here is 'relevant'. It is not about finding the largest possible number of interactions – that way leads to confusion and contradiction – it is about finding those interactions that match precisely with the customer's aspirations and expectations.

162

An ideal tool for the task has of course already been discussed at some length in this chapter – the *customer activity cycle* (see Figure 9.1).

It is interesting to see how this most versatile of tools is used to *complete* the brand positioning process, while being the *first* step of the value creation process with individual customers. What this illustrates is an important continuum in the matching process described in this chapter, moving from the 'big picture' – the supplier's brand matching with the market – to the 'small picture' – the supplier matching with their most important customers through a 1:1 collaborative relationship.

Part IV

Aligning

10

The critical success factors

FROM CONCEPTION TO BIRTH, AND BEYOND...

Creating value is rather like creating life. In Chapter 9 we discussed the point at which the creation of value begins: working between supplier and customer the *customer activity cycle* shows us the clues and the possibilities and the positive impact analysis helps us to make our choice. We might think of this as the point of conception.

Now the supplier sets to work through the collaborative processes within their own organization. This is the hard part – making it happen – and we might think of this as the period of gestation.

The delivery of this new value back to the customer is of course the moment of birth. But it doesn't finish there. The supplier and customer are parents to a new child, now they must make sure that it grows up to fulfil its potential. We want our value to make good.

Parts II and III have dealt largely with analytical processes; how to focus on the right customers and how to match their needs – two sides of the value machine triangle.

Such things are easy enough to do. Whether they are implemented with any lasting positive effect is of course another thing altogether.

In the three chapters of Part 4 we will deal with making it happen – addressing those periods of gestation, birth and growing up. This is the task of aligning the business (the third side of the value machine triangle) in a way

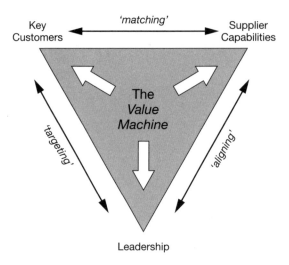

Figure 10.1 *The value machine triangle*

that aims to make lasting practical use out of our work in focusing and matching, and here we arrive at the point of 'make or break' – the people.

People will either facilitate these processes, ignore them, or get in their way. Unfortunately, the last of these three is all too common, not from any malicious intent, but simply because there are other processes already in place – why change?

It will be clear by now that creating a value machine is no easy task, but just in case you were feeling complacent this chapter will start by painting the task in its gloomiest colours, listing some of the most common obstacles that stand in the way. They exist in the majority of businesses, sometimes quite naturally, sometimes self-inflicted.

Once we know what we are up against we will turn to a discussion of the '*critical success factors*'; the things that we need to have in place, to be good at, and to focus on for achieving a well-oiled and effective value machine.

SINS AND OBSTACLES

The following list of 'sins' is compiled after many years of encountering pretty much the same obstacles most everywhere I go. If many of them resonate with you and your organization then I must leave it to you whether this commonality makes you feel better (for not being alone), or more depressed (for not being better). The good news is that all of them can be dealt with, given a strong enough will at the top married with the appropriate leadership style and actions, meaning: attention to the people issues:

- inertia and complacency;
- unclear or conflicting goals;
- short-termism – including abandoning the concept in times of crisis;
- the 'silo mentality', with business/function managers as 'barons';
- clashes of objectives and priorities across functions;
- taking on too many Key or Key Development Accounts;
- inadequate customer distinction – no plan for 'freeing up the energy';
- inadequate authority given to customer teams;
- cross-functional team working is a rare (or untried) experience;
- coaching skills are under-used or under-represented;
- the sales team have a preference for 'independence' and loan 'hunting';
- 'internal' staff have low confidence or skills in customer contact;
- a non 'streetwise' 'internal' team;
- no experience of collaborative partnering with customers;
- existing IT systems no longer appropriate but too deeply embedded to change… ;
- customer planning owned exclusively by the sales team;
- inadequate (or no) measures of customer profitability;
- no process for assessing and comparing investment propositions.

That the role of leadership in tackling these obstacles is one of the critical success factors goes almost without saying; you will see it at the top of the list in the following section, but we will save a fuller discussion on this until the final chapter – a suitable place to close.

For now, just one comment on the leadership role will help set a tone of reality for the rest of this chapter. In taking on these kind of obstacles, in any complex organization, there is a need for a high sense of political awareness: what is necessary, what is possible, and what just has to do for now? It is not necessary to cure everything all at once; it is not even necessary to cure everything. You will know from your own experience which sins present the biggest obstacles in your business and which need tackling first, last, or not at all.

THE CRITICAL SUCCESS FACTORS (CSFS)

The following is not an attempt at an exhaustive list, nor does it necessarily comprise the most important CSFs (that list can only depend on your own circumstances). It is instead a 'typical list', based on the requirements that I have most commonly seen in businesses aiming to implement a value machine business strategy:

- the ability to lead change (see Chapter 12);
- a strong culture of coaching and empowerment (see Chapter 12);
- clarity of our own business drivers and money-making logic (see below);
- a robust planning process and application toolkit:
  - the planning funnel (see Chapter 3);
  - segmentation, customer classification and customer distinction (see Chapters 4 and 5);
  - Diamond Team contact management (see Chapter 6);
  - value creation – the customer activity cycle (see Chapter 9).
- cross-functional alignment with strong functional excellence (see below);
- cross-functional supplier team working (see Chapter 11);
- customer collaboration (see Chapter 11):
  - interpersonal skills;
  - commercial awareness;
  - legal and contractual acuity;
  - project management.
- Key Account Management processes (see below);
- the measurement of customer profitability (see below).

Some of these CSFs have been discussed already (chapter references are noted in the list). Chapter 11 will address the tasks of building *cross-functional supplier* teams and developing healthy *customer collaboration*, and Chapter 12 will address the tasks of *leading change*, and developing a *strong culture of coaching and empowerment*.

As with the obstacles, you will know which of these critical success factors are the most urgent in your own circumstances, and which might even be regarded as simply 'nice to haves'. Don't attempt everything all at once!

CLARITY OF BUSINESS DRIVERS AND MONEY-MAKING LOGIC

The tools for assessing the customer's business strategy discussed in Chapter 8 can of course be applied to the supplier's own business. How do you aim to grow (Ansoff Matrix), how do you aim to compete (Porter's choices), what values drive your business (Wiersema) and what is your money-making logic? We won't elaborate on them again, but instead ask one pertinent question and make two important observations.

First, the question: must a business operating to the principles of the value machine be led by Wiersema's *Customer Intimacy* driver? The principle of matching makes it seem so, as does the intention to modify internal processes based on what is learned through that matching process. So does this exclude any businesses driven principally by *Operational Excellence* or *Product Leadership* from the value machine club? No, not at all, absolutely not. The nature of your business drivers should determine the nature of your value machine, and not the other way around.

If *Operational Excellence* is vital to you as either a source of competitive advantage or as a key plank of your money-making logic, then you will be looking for customer opportunities that both value your OE and promise to enhance it. This will determine the nature of your matching process and so the nature of your value machine.

Likewise if *Product Leadership* is the vital driver in your business, the customer opportunities sought will be those that value your PL and might enhance it. What we see going on here is in fact a very effective way of selecting the right opportunities and making the right investments.

Now for the two observations. First, it can only serve to help if we use the same tools and language to analyse our customer's business strategy as we do to define our own. To repeat a point made in Chapter 8, this is not because we aim for the same strategy as them, rather, we aim to be relevant, and to make a positive impact, and to gain the appropriate reward for ourselves. A uniform language is going to be helpful in the task of matching and selecting the priority opportunities, and will become almost essential as we move towards the forging of collaborative partnerships.

The second observation is: given the way in which our choice of lead driver and our money-making logic will influence the nature of our value machine it is very important that these choices are crystal clear, communicated effectively and agreed by all involved. This was the third CSF on our list above, and takes us neatly to the fifth: ensuring cross-functional alignment.

CROSS-FUNCTIONAL ALIGNMENT AND FUNCTIONAL EXCELLENCE

Business structure

Is this about company structure and organization – the lines on the charts – or is it about attitudes and behaviours? I rather favour the latter (and plenty more will be said on this later in this chapter and in Chapters 11 and 12). I have rarely seen change driven simply by a reorganization of functional titles and reporting lines. When such changes do appear to be successful it is usually because the real changes have already happened, behind the scenes as it were. The people concerned were already trying to work in different ways and the restructuring was actioned in order to remove their frustrations.

That said, there are some organizational structures that are just going to be difficult, full stop. The classic problem structure is reproduced in Figure 10.2.

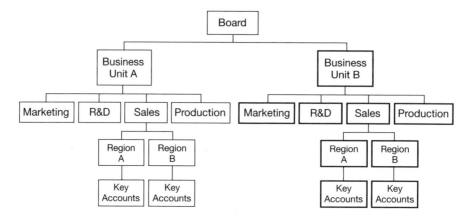

Figure 10.2 *Silo-based structures*

The silo structure is the mortal enemy of the value machine – what we might call a 'no chance' structure. Of course it *can* work, if all the heads of the functions are on board, and all are happy to facilitate cross-functional working beneath them, and to do this without concerns over budgets, or people's time allocation, or the measurement of departmental performance... OK, we see the problem.

If customer/supplier teams are to be truly cross-functional, if the functions are to be aligned behind a customer-focused vision, if the returns on our investments (budgets!) are to be measured across the whole business, and if the business decision-making processes are to be driven by customer collaboration, then isn't all of that going to turn the organization upside down? For sure, so why not just do it?

Figure 10.3 compares a traditional hierarchy and a value machine hierarchy, simply turning the organization upside down.

In traditional hierarchies the management sit at the top and the people with customer contact sit lower down, often at the bottom. In a value machine hierarchy the people with customer contact are placed right at the top, with the lines of management beneath. If you can't be rid of the functional silos then at least turn them in the direction of the customer.

We haven't actually changed the company structure, all the organization charts remain the same, but we have made a very important symbolic point, and one that is designed to change attitudes and behaviours.

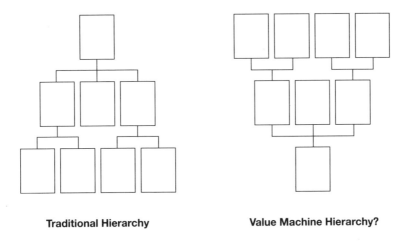

Traditional Hierarchy   **Value Machine Hierarchy?**

Figure 10.3 *The organization turned upside down*

I once worked for one of the UKs largest companies, a conglomerate of monster proportions where silos abounded and traditional hierarchies were the order of the day. One fine day a new divisional manager arrived and was intent on change. Gathering the leadership team together he addressed us with some pointed questions:

'Who in this room has contact with customers?'

Some of us were sales managers, so we put our hands up.

'Not many I see. How many of you support people who have contact with customers?'

We all sat on our hands – we were managers after all.

'Right. From now on this will be our new structure,' and he tore down the traditional silo organogram from the wall and replaced it, upside down. Then he turned on us: 'And if you don't have direct contact with customers, and if you don't support someone who does, then you have no place in this new organization.'

We got the message. The structure remained in place but our attitudes and behaviours started changing fast. And then guess what? We started to empower people, and to change the nature of their performance measures. We started to encourage more cross-functional working. We started to get frustrated as the structure got in the way, so now we changed the structure to match what was now going on for real in the business.

The correct structure for a value machine must be one that allows us to match the customers' aspirations while working to our own positive benefit. It is not possible to describe such a structure in any more detail given that it must be dependent on so many matters of particular circumstance. We can only talk in principles.

One such principle is to ensure that your structure is relevant to your key customers. Such customers will have little sympathy for structures that mean something to the supplier but have no positive benefit for them. Worse, they might see such structures as obstacles to true collaboration. It is interesting to note that whereas in the past a good supplier would always try to secure the customer's structure chart it is now quite normal for a customer to ask their supplier to provide details and explanations of their structure. The customer is just as keen to test the possibilities of collaboration as is the supplier. If they see something resembling the structure illustrated in Figure 10.2 what do you imagine they are going to conclude?

Evolution rather than revolution is usually another good principle when it comes to business structure. Revolutions usually risk losing much of what was good in what went before. If the occasional radical shake-up is required, then that is probably only because the business has failed to evolve its structure over time as it should have done. Figure 10.4 shows how a structure might evolve over time.

We see the move from a typical country-based structure where business units play a secondary role to one where the business units lead but the country element has not disappeared entirely. Over time 'channels' begin to be more important, replacing countries as the secondary element, and over further time they swap places with the business units as the structural driving force. Under a channel-driven structure individual Key Accounts start to rise to prominence as elements in the structure, and it is easy to see how this may morph once more towards Key Account-led structures, if that is a requirement. A value machine must develop in similar ways – evolution not revolution.

Any business that is responsive to their markets will already have structural elements that have been 'prompted' by their customers. If the market demands low and steadily decreasing prices then a supplier structure that helps promote cost reduction will have developed to facilitate that, with manufacturing very likely taking a prominent role. If the market demands high-tech products with 'added value' services, then we might expect to find R&D in a more 'forward' position, and a structure in R&D that facilitates close collaboration with the sales team, or maybe even directly with the customer.

Might we take this further, and aim to develop our structure in line with our approach to customer classification and customer distinction (see Chapter 5), perhaps as shown in Figure 10.4? This may be a bridge too far, or you may be on the cusp of a breakthrough – it depends on so many variables that general comments are not helpful, other than to say you might give the notion some thought. Perhaps a step in this direction could be to modify the measures of performance used in the different functions, to be in line with our customer classification and distinction strategies.

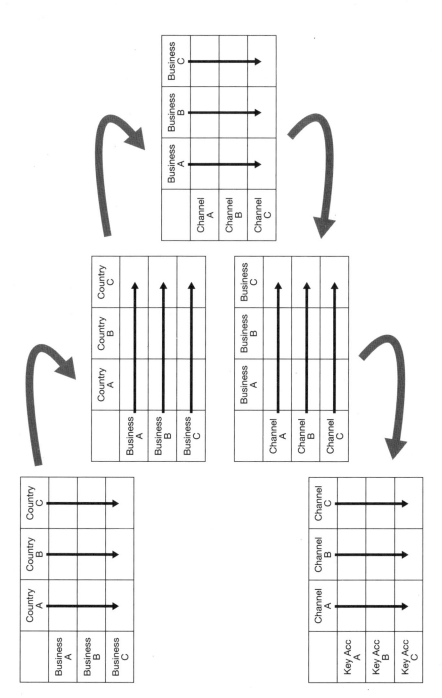

Figure 10.4 *The evolving structure*

PERFORMANCE MANAGEMENT MEASURES

There is no doubt that one of the biggest obstacles to cross-functional alignment is the existence of different and sometimes conflicting performance management measures. A production manager might be measured on 'occupacity' – a good OE measure that looks for the efficiency with which they use the plant to ensure maximum output. A Key Account Manager might approach that manager with a 'customer focused' request – to produce a modified product. Let's say that this might involve closing the production line, a re-tooling, a relatively short production run, another close down, another re-tooling, and then back to where we left off. Should the Key Account Manager be surprised if the Production Manager sends them packing?

Perhaps the solution is to be found in the world of professional basketball? Anyone that follows professional basketball will know about the host of statistics that surround the game. There seems to be a measure for every single aspect. Players' performances are measured with merciless accuracy – that is the nature of the professional game. Two measures stand out – 'baskets' and 'assists', that is, how many times they put the ball through the hoop, and how many times their 'play' helped another player put the ball through the hoop. Couldn't some functions be measured on 'assists'? If the aim of the business is to deal with more customer-focused orders, implying shorter runs and smaller batches, then would it be better to measure the Production Manager by their speed in changing products rather than their occupacity? This has the enormous benefit of allowing that Production Manager to retain an *Operationally Excellent* measure appropriate to their function while operating in a *Customer Intimate* environment. This brings us to the question of functional excellence, and another important principle.

FUNCTIONAL EXCELLENCE

I'm going to assume that each function within your business knows how to run their own affairs, in so far as they impact 'on themselves' and the 'next function in line'. This is usually so, and will save me teaching grandmothers to suck eggs...

We will focus on just one vital rule, and a rule that sits at the heart of any great value machine – the concept that each function knows best, and the least interference from others the better. If this sounds worryingly like the promotion of silos with island mentalities, just what we are aiming to avoid, then please read to the end before you come to your own conclusion.

Way back in Chapter 3 I asked: if only sales reps would stop and think once in a while like distribution people, and if only distribution people would occasionally think like sales reps – wouldn't that get things done a little bit more effectively? The essential phrases were 'once in a while' and 'occasionally'…

Functions are usually at their best when allowed to operate to the high professional standards of their own disciplines. Start asking them to be all things to all men, or to mimic the disciplines and processes of other functions and they can easily lose their way. Ask sales people to improve their 'occupacity' and you will soon be into the wasteful foolishness of call rates and coverage. Ask an R&D department to 'close more deals' and you will fast be looking at a department personified by facile mediocrity.

What we seek is functional excellence within the context of the value machine. All functions must be aligned behind the same customer-focused strategy, and take care not to allow them the easy way out by saying that they serve 'internal customers'. Such weasel words have too often allowed functions to ignore their impact on the real customer, hiding from their responsibilities behind a shield of the next function along. All functions have an impact on the customer, in the end, and they should know what it is, and how to ensure that it is a good one.

All functions must work towards the goal of enhanced value propositions that benefit both customer and supplier. Again, no weasel words about internal customers, each function must know their value to the customer, and each function must know their positive impact on their own business.

If we have these things, then allowing each function to operate as they know to be best – by their own lights but in pursuit of the common goal – is always going to prove the most effective approach.

This will not come without disputes and occasional turf wars. We might even expect to see an increase in these things in the short term as functions are expected to work in closer collaboration; the teething problems of new neighbours. Collaboration doesn't necessarily mean harmony; some of the best collaborative efforts – 'best' meaning as judged by their outcomes – can be very stormy indeed. Think of all those great comic duos, or legendary rock bands, where the people involved couldn't wait to get away from each other after the show, and yet consider what they achieved when they were together. Why should business people be any different – do we not have egos, and feelings?

THE RIGHT ATTITUDES

What contributes most to success in aligning functions is not the structures but the attitudes. The great musical groups of any era have been great not because there were rules about who played what, or who stood where, or who wrote and who performed and who made the tea, but because the members wanted to work together – they saw the benefits of their collaboration and they were pleased by the outcomes. Take away these last two points and the collaboration folds.

Let's take a more mundane case, that of a sales professional who needs to chase the right kinds of order to facilitate an operationally excellent driven manufacturing company. What constitutes 'right'? Well, it depends. If the factory is full then big orders gained by heavy discounting are not going to help, but if the factory is working at low occupacity then such an order might be just the thing. So, the sales people need to know about the state of the factory, and what it requires at any time for optimal working. You might aim to achieve that by putting the sales team under the responsibility of the production department, taking their instruction from the plant manager and having their sales processes determined by the people in operations – though I think you will agree that this structural solution is going to be fraught with problems. Surely it is better to give the sales team access to up-to-date information on the state of the plant, encourage them to use it by linking their performance measures to their impact on the plant, and then let them get on with the sales process itself as they know best?

KEY ACCOUNT MANAGEMENT PROCESSES

This is a big subject and I am tempted to refer you to my own book on the huge range of challenges and issues – *Key Account Management*, also published by Kogan Page – and just move right on to the next topic. Tempted, but not succumbing. The following is in no way an attempt to describe KAM as a whole. I will ignore huge slices of its principles and practices (painful though that is to one who thinks KAM is the most fun you can have with your clothes on), discussing it only in so far as it is an integral part of the value machine, benefiting from its principles and processes and contributing towards its successes.

There are five critical requirements (CSFs within the CSFs):

1.   The Key and Key Development Accounts should be identified through a robust process of customer classification, as described in Chapter 5, the selection criteria being shared across the whole business and chosen as relevant to the business strategy and objectives.
2.   There should not be too many Key and Key Development Accounts. True customer collaboration is very time and resource consuming – better to focus on a few and manage them brilliantly than on too many with the

almost inevitable mediocre outcomes.

3.   The practice of KAM must be managed through cross-functional teams, supported at senior levels, with shared objectives and responsibilities that supersede those of individual functions or departments – the _Diamond Teams_ described in Chapter 6.

4.   KA Teams must have the capabilities and resources to identify value propositions relevant to the customer's processes and business strategies – this calls for particular skills within the teams, it requires the use of some key tools (the _customer activity cycle_ for one – see Chapter 9), but most importantly it will only result from those involved having sufficient time available.

5.   KA teams must have sufficient authority (and skill) to develop the chosen value propositions through carefully managed investment projects and a process of customer collaboration.

Does this call for a new breed of Key Account Managers? Perhaps it does. The old model of promoted sales representatives will almost certainly struggle in this new environment. What is really needed are Key Account Managers who are a combination of business managers, team leaders, coaches and project managers. If they happen also to be great sales people then fine, but better to find the right KA Manager based on these criteria and then give them some professional sales expertise _within_ their team than see a great sales professional struggle with the other requirements.

MEASURING CUSTOMER PROFITABILITY

I confess that this is something of a soapbox of mine. It frustrates me that this is so clearly essential to the health of the process and yet is something still so little done. Perhaps I should be more understanding of the problems involved, or perhaps I should just stay on my soapbox – this is a must do CSF!

The aim of the value machine is a more effective and efficient use of our business resources focused on a carefully classified customer base. So why isn't measuring total profitability enough? Because the value machine sinks or swims based on a few very carefully chosen investments with Key or Key Development Accounts, and we should know how those investments are performing. What if we have made the wrong choices? What if the costs (significant but 'unseen' when building 'collaborative relationships') are outrunning the returns? Things have a way of running out of control...

Consider the tale of the UK's National Health Service. Created in the 1940s the NHS was heralded not only as a mark of a new height of civilization, but also as a route to greater efficiency. The planners sincerely believed that the NHS would result in the steadily decreasing cost of healthcare provision. Why? Because the NHS would improve the health of the nation – the populace would therefore require 'less healthcare'.

We now know how things turned out in practice – people expected ever-more sophisticated treatments for an apparently ever-growing range of ailments. It was almost as if the NHS invented a whole new range of diseases!

Is it possible that the creation of *Diamond Teams* (aiming to work in close collaboration with customers, in pursuit of enhanced value for the customer and greater effectiveness and efficiency for the supplier) might in themselves uncover a never-ending range of new needs, opportunities and actions required? It is to be hoped so, but should we suppose that each one of these new opportunities is as good for us as the last?

Might the analogy with the NHS continue further – the health of the nation really *did* improve, but as the demands on it increased so costs began to spiral out of control resulting in NHS Trusts getting into serious financial difficulties. In the end the government had to impose 'value for money' measurements based on how any particular drug or treatment contributed to the patient's quality of life. Sometimes it was considered just too expensive to extend a patient's life another six months, or to ameliorate their suffering by '10 per cent'.

The newspapers had a field day of course – peoples' lives and NHS return on investment calculations seemed very uncomfortable bedfellows when presented in that way – as indeed they are, when presented in this way. With the powers of hindsight perhaps it would have helped had the NHS always worked in such a way, with patient expectations managed from the start?

Such dangers can be avoided in our own businesses if we aim to measure customer profitability *from the start*.

Here are four 'almost truths' (that is to say, they are very nearly always so) of customer profitability:

1. The largest customers (ranked by volume) are rarely the same as the most profitable customers (measured by percentage return on investment).
2. The costs of working in close collaboration with customers, particularly new customers, even in a high-growth environment, are almost always higher than you think…
3. The longer you keep a customer the more profitable it should become.

4.	Customer profitability extends beyond the individual customer P&L – consideration should also be taken of the way a customer's business might improve our efficiency (perhaps through economies of scale) or our effectiveness (perhaps by developing a new capability).

Without proper measures of profitability it is all too easy to favour 'big customers' simply for their size, and far too easy to plunge into costly customer collaborations without thought of the consequences – I call this the sin of _collaborative ooze_, things just, well, ooze…

Big customers cost more to work with and service than middle-sized ones. They get better prices, better terms and more attention. Perhaps this is compensated by economies of scale, or by improvements to our own processes and capabilities, but we really ought to know if that is really so, or just an act of faith.

Development customers cost more to work with than we know or measure. There are the costs of trials, of free stock used in pilot exercises, of people's time and travel, the costs of project team presentations and reviews. Improving our own capabilities throughout such a process is good, but doesn't necessarily come free – there might be new systems to install, staff training or new operating procedures. We might also factor in the costs of taking those people away from other projects and activities – what if while directing your best people to a new Key Development Account you take your eye off the ball and lose an existing piece of business with another customer? Enough 'what ifs', wouldn't it be better just to measure profitability from the start?

The longer you keep a customer the more profitable it _should_ become… and note well the use of the word 'should'. The reasons are many; the benefits of the _experience curve_ where suppliers grow more expert over time, improving efficiencies, the highlighting of new opportunities as relationships mature and improve, the benefits brought to other customers through improved capabilities and effectiveness. It has even been calculated that if a manufacturing company can improve its retention rate (how long it keeps its customers) by only 5 per cent it will see a 45 per cent increase in profitability, while an insurance company might see an 84 per cent increase for the same improvement in retention and an advertising agency as much as 95 per cent (see FA Reichheld, quoted in _Relationship Marketing For Competitive Advantage_, eds A Payne, M Christopher, M Clark and H Peck).

A key benefit of long-term relationships, key to the working of the value machine, is the way that our greater experience allows us to make better investment choices. Figure 10.5 shows a comparison of two circumstances – the first based on poor experience and knowledge (let's say the result of inadequate _Bow-tie_ relationships (see Chapter 6) with customers) and the second based on the enhanced knowledge resulting from _Diamond Team_ relationships.

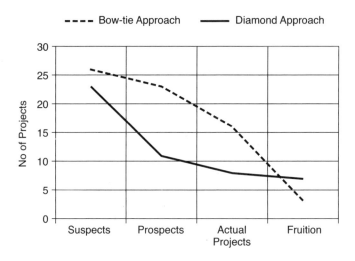

Figure 10.5 *The benefits of experience*

In the first case the business feels obliged to chase all new opportunities that come its way, and with inevitable results – many of them fall by the wayside. The return on investment is poor because of so much wasted effort along the way. In the second case the business is in a much better position to make its judgements and chooses rather better which horses to back. Even if the same number of horses (sorry, projects) make it to the winning line, the return on investment will be much better in the second case through better use of resources in the first place.

Sometimes the paybacks expected from long-term relationships are themselves rather long term and that is part of the problem for measuring customer profitability particularly in businesses obsessed by their annual reports. Part of the value machine philosophy should perhaps be to measure customer profitability over the longer term, what we might call the *lifetime value* of a customer. This would certainly allow us to build-in more readily some of those 'fringe benefits' of customer referrals and the like.

Whether measured over the short or the long term, it is certainly important to make an attempt to include all related costs, to go further than the simple gross margin resulting from sales revenue minus materials.

Consider the tale of the 'marmalader', that is to say, a business that attempts to measure customer profitability by spreading all overhead costs 'evenly' across all customers regardless of actual use. Figure 10.6 shows the starting point of this business.

Customers	A	B	C	D	Total
Gross Profit	100	80	60	50	290
Overheads	60	60	60	60	240
Net Profit	40	20	0	(10)	50

Figure 10.6 _The sins of marmalading – part 1_

Let us suppose that the business has four customers with a combined gross profit of 290 and shows a net profit of 50. The marmalading of the 240-worth of overheads indicates a loss-making customer – customer D. The decision is taken to cease doing business with that customer.

Unfortunately, overheads do not reduce immediately by the 60 units that had been allocated to customer D. But perhaps they do go down by 30 and people give themselves a slap on the back for a smart decision. The new situation is now as shown in Figure 10.7.

Customers	A	B	C	D	Total
Gross Profit	_100_	_80_	_60_	_50_	_290_
Overheads	_60_	_60_	_60_	_60_	_240_
Net Profit	_40_	_20_	_0_	_(10)_	_50_
Gross Profit	100	80	60	xx	240
Overheads	70	70	70	xx	210
Net Profit	30	10	(10)	xx	30

Figure 10.7 _The sins of marmalading – part 2_

Once again the overheads are spread 'evenly' and while the business is still in profit (albeit a lower one) we now find that customer C is apparently a loss-maker. The troubled board meets to decide action. 'Concentrate on profitable customers', they say, and customer C is quietly dropped. But, unfortunately, the overheads do not reduce in line, as demonstrated by the new situation shown in Figure 10.8.

Customers	A	B	C	D	Total
Gross Profit	_100_	_80_	_60_	_50_	_290_
Overheads	_60_	_60_	_60_	_60_	_240_
Net Profit	_40_	_20_	_0_	_(10)_	_50_
Gross Profit	_100_	_80_	_60_	_xx_	_240_
Overheads	_70_	_70_	_70_	_xx_	_210_
Net Profit	_30_	_10_	_(10)_	_xx_	_30_
Gross Profit	100	80	xx	xx	180
Overheads	90	90	xx	xx	180
Net Profit	10	(10)	xx	xx	0

Figure 10.8 _The sins of marmalading – part 3_

I think you can guess what happens next.

Perhaps their salvation lay in some form of *activity-based costing* where the true costs of overheads are allocated to individual customers as they are utilized. From there, *cost-to-serve* models can be created, showing how customers compare across the spectrum of costs and returns. Yes it is complicated, and no it is rarely precise, but surely it is better than not knowing at all? In fact, the effort to create such models often raises unknown facts about our business and its money-making logic, facts that we can feed into our business planning funnel as discussed in Chapter 3 (see Figure 3.1) – and so we come full circle.

Getting cross-functional teams to work

There is no better place for a cross-functional team to learn and develop than on the job. The *customer activity cycle* (see Chapter 9) is almost certainly the best way to pool corporate knowledge and send it into action. The *supporters' and opponents'* tool (see Chapter 7) is probably the best for setting off 'constructive arguments'. It will be by working through these kind of analytical and application tools, by taking on their responsibilities for seeking out and then pooling their knowledge, and by getting stuck into the nitty-gritty of application alongside colleagues and customer, that teams will grow and prosper. The problem is getting them to this stage.

Once the experience has been tried, and more importantly once the benefits start to flow, there is almost no stopping such teams. This chapter aims to get what might still yet be notional teams to this happy state of self-propelled effectiveness, and then it's over to them.

Earlier chapters have touched on some helpful steps, such as the drawing up of G.R.O.W.s to include in the Contact Matrix, as described in Chapter 7. Such things are essential processes but our main focus in this chapter will be on facilitating the human side of such internal collaborations. Three tools will be discussed: *Belbin's Team Roles*, the idea of the *Team Clock* and the role of the *Team Leader*.

Once internal collaboration is achieved we must move on to customer collaboration, and here we will consider four areas of importance: the need for highly developed *interpersonal skills* across the whole supplier team (not just the sales force), the need for high levels of *commercial awareness* (the 'streetwise' team), the need for *legal and contractual acuity* when exposed to the customer's environment, and a robust process for *project management*.

SOME ADVICE...

Here are four simple pieces of advice that will help (or at least give you some solace) in what can be a sometimes frustrating journey towards truly effective teams. They might have the ring of 'motherhood and apple pie' about them – platitudes if you like – but they remain sound advice for all that.

First, tackle things step by step. The first meeting of a new cross-functional team will not get very far – people will be nervous, suspicious, sceptical, cynical and most other things to boot – this is not the time or place for agreeing G.R.O.W.s or encouraging debates, however constructive you may intend them to be.

Second, have enormous reserves of patience, but be persistent, and remember your goals at all times.

Third, celebrate progress, however small, and as loudly as is seemly in the circumstances.

And finally, know when to stop. Perfection isn't possible, nor desirable given the likely efforts required to achieve it. Learn to forgive the occasional weaknesses in others – they may just reciprocate.

BELBIN'S TEAM ROLES

When forming a cross-functional team most people will think, naturally enough, about the functions first. People's roles are to be determined by their department, their job title and their seniority. While this makes good logical sense it may not in fact be the best place to start. Teams are about people first and foremost, and so it is with the people that we should begin. This is the beauty of the work of Dr Meredith Belbin who has developed a robust and well-proven model for team working based on people's contribution to teams *as people* – what Dr Belbin calls their 'team roles'.

There are nine roles identified in the Belbin model, each having a distinct and valuable contribution to make to the successful working of the whole team. Each role has its positive qualities, and also what Belbin calls its allowable weakness – the price you pay for the strength. Figures 11.1 through to 11.9 summarize each of these roles.

THE *COORDINATOR'S* CONTRIBUTION
- Coordinates the way the team moves towards group objectives
- Makes best use of team resources
- Recognizes team strengths and weaknesses
- Maximizes the potential of each team member through encouragement
- Acts as a focal point for group effort in tough times

POSITIVE QUALITIES
- Welcomes all contributions on their merit
- Listens without prejudice, remains focused on the main objective
- The team's ringmaster

ALLOWABLE WEAKNESSES
- Is unlikely to be the most creative member of the team

WHAT TO WATCH OUT FOR
- Obstinacy vs determination

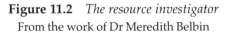

Figure 11.1 *The coordinator*
From the work of Dr Meredith Belbin

THE *RESOURCE INVESTIGATOR'S* CONTRIBUTION
- Explores and reports on ideas and developments outside the team
- Creates external contacts
- The best person to set up external contacts

POSITIVE QUALITIES
- Capacity for contacting people and exploring anything new
- Enthusiasm and a source of external ideas
- Ability to respond to challenge
- The team's detective

ALLOWABLE WEAKNESSES
- Low boredom threshold, needs stimulus of others, may spend time on irrelevancies

WHAT TO WATCH OUT FOR
- Too much involvement in own ideas rather than those of the team

Figure 11.2 *The resource investigator*
From the work of Dr Meredith Belbin

THE *SHAPER'S* CONTRIBUTION
- Directs the way in which team effort is channelled
- Focuses attention on objectives and priorities
- Results-oriented and competitive
- Pushing through change

POSITIVE QUALITIES
- A readiness to challenge politics and inertia
- Tough on complacency and self-deception
- The architect of the team

ALLOWABLE WEAKNESSES
- Prone to provocation, irritation and impatience

WHAT TO WATCH OUT FOR
- Arrogance and pushiness
- Steamrolling colleagues into a course of action

Figure 11.3   *The shaper*
From the work of Dr Meredith Belbin

THE *COMPLETER FINISHER'S* CONTRIBUTION
- Ensures nothing has been overlooked
- Checks details
- Maintains a sense of urgency
- Invaluable where accuracy and deadlines are important

POSITIVE QUALITIES
- Capacity for follow-through
- High standards in quality and delivery
- The team's workhorse

ALLOWABLE WEAKNESSES
- Tendency to worry about small things
- Reluctant to let go

WHAT TO WATCH OUT FOR
- Getting bogged down in details

Figure 11.4   *The completer finisher*
From the work of Dr Meredith Belbin

THE *IMPLEMENTER'S* CONTRIBUTION

- Turns concepts and plans into practical working procedures – does what has to be done
- Carries out agreed plans systematically and efficiently

POSITIVE QUALITIES

- Organizing ability, practical common sense
- Self-disciplined, hard-working, trustworthy
- The process controller of the team

ALLOWABLE WEAKNESSES

- Lack of flexibility, unresponsive to new or unproven ideas

WHAT TO WATCH OUT FOR

- Criticizing others for their lack of pragmatism
- Getting stuck in a rut

Figure 11.5 *The implementer*

From the work of Dr Meredith Belbin

THE *MONITOR EVALUATOR'S* CONTRIBUTION

- Analyses problems, evaluates ideas and suggestions
- Enables the team to take balanced decisions
- Checks and balances

POSITIVE QUALITIES

- Judgement, objectivity, discretion, hard-headedness
- The team's conscience

ALLOWABLE WEAKNESSES

- May lack inspiration and ability to motivate others
- Can appear aloof and even negative

WHAT TO WATCH OUT FOR

- Criticizing others too frequently
- Lack of awareness of the big picture

Figure 11.6 *The monitor evaluator*

From the work of Dr Meredith Belbin

189

THE *TEAM WORKER'S* CONTRIBUTION
- Supports other team members
- Builds on suggestions
- Compensates for other team members' shortcomings
- Fosters a team spirit
- Ensures internal communications are kept up

POSITIVE QUALITIES
- Ability to respond to people and situations
- Enthusiasm
- The team's 'glue'

ALLOWABLE WEAKNESSES
- Indecisive, especially under pressure

WHAT TO WATCH OUT FOR
- Stress, especially within internally competitive teams

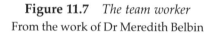

Figure 11.7   *The team worker*

From the work of Dr Meredith Belbin

THE *PLANT'S* CONTRIBUTION
- New ideas and creativity
- A creative approach to problem solving
- Challenging the status quo

POSITIVE QUALITIES
- Lateral thinking
- The 'spark' of the team

ALLOWABLE WEAKNESSES
- Inclined to disregard processes and protocols

WHAT TO WATCH OUT FOR
- Handling criticism badly – switching off
- Becoming an ivory tower

Figure 11.8   *The plant*

From the work of Dr Meredith Belbin

THE *SPECIALIST'S* CONTRIBUTION
• Specific skills and work-related capabilities

POSITIVE QUALITIES
• High level of functional skill and knowledge
• Professional standards
• Commitment
• Pride in their work

ALLOWABLE WEAKNESSES
• Lack of interest in other's roles

WHAT TO WATCH OUT FOR
• Can become too single minded
• Slow to change if their specialization is threatened

Figure 11.9 *The specialist*
From the work of Dr Meredith Belbin

The 'ideal' team will need to contain all roles, but that does not mean you need a team of nine – each team member will probably display two, or maybe three of the roles as the leading roles within their make-up and personality.

A simple questionnaire can help the team identify the roles most likely to be played by each member, and once that is done a little analysis should follow. Figure 11.10 gives a sample team profile ready for discussion – the circles mark the lead roles of each individual, and the conspicuous absence of any particular role across the team.

Belbin Team Role	RS	BD	JR	KC	LM	TP			Total
Completer Finisher	3	8	(13)	0	(14)	7			
Implementer	5	(11)	8	8	0	5			
Monitor Evaluator	3	6	4	6	4	7			◯
Specialist	0	4	(11)	5	6	0			
Coordinator	(14)	8	8	(16)	(13)	(18)			
Team Worker	2	6	7	9	7	10			◯
Resource Investigator	2	(11)	6	(12)	7	5			
Shaper	(27)	3	9	10	(13)	(13)			
Plant	2	3	6	4	4	5			◯

Figure 11.10 *Sample Belbin team profile*
From the work of Dr Meredith Belbin

191

- What roles, if any, are missing, or under-represented?
  - What will be the implication of that on team performance?
  - What can you do to compensate?
- What roles are 'abundant', perhaps even over-represented?
  - What will be the implication of that on team performance?
  - What can you do to mitigate that?

The absence of a *Plant* is quite common (so many company selection processes work to exclude such 'mavericks') – and a possible solution might be to arrange for the temporary importation of such a person when such behaviour is required. Failing that, the team might like to make use of some deliberate 'creative thinking' tools for some part of their meetings. (I have plenty to recommend – see 'Getting further help'.)

The absence of a *Monitor Evaluator* might call for a team rule: before concluding on anything, let's always have an 'are we certain/have we checked' session... particularly important in a team dominated by *Shapers* and *Completer Finishers* who will be certain about the plan and wanting to rush off to get things done!

Any absence is a problem, and what is certainly *not* advised is that the team simply look for the highest-scoring individual for that role (regardless of the fact that it ranks low in their own profile) and expects them to provide the goods. The result will only be an increase in stress for that individual as they are forced to play out a suboptimal scenario.

Over-abundance is another kind of problem. A group of perfectly cloned *Team Workers* might get on well together – peace and harmony will reign – but it is doubtful that they will ever complete the task in hand. Too many *Shapers* is a common outcome (though sometimes this is about people *wanting* to be Shapers just as much as really being *Shapers*), and by simply recognizing this over-abundance the team is already better placed to deal with the almost inevitable 'friction' to come. This is one of the great benefits of the Belbin model; allowing individuals to recognize their own behaviours and discuss them openly using a language that avoids personal criticism.

I wouldn't advise going through a Belbin exercise at the first meeting of a new team – get to know each other a little first, good and bad, and then when you do go through the analysis at some later stage the discussion will be far more fruitful. The discussion is key, don't aim to squeeze this into a half-hour session 'between the important stuff' – this is the important stuff. The good news is that people like talking about themselves, and this gives them the perfect excuse!

THE TEAM CLOCK

You are perhaps already familiar with the terms 'forming', 'storming', 'norming' and 'performing', as applied to team working? Figure 11.11 illustrates these four stages of team development around a clock face.

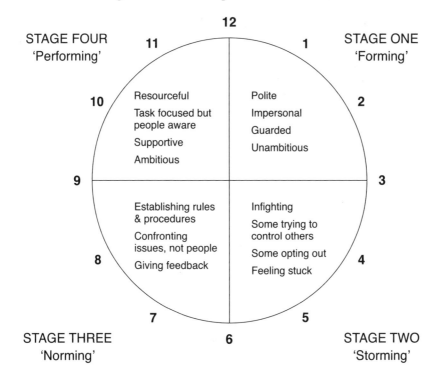

Figure 11.11   *The team clock*

All teams must go through these four stages, from initial 'forming', where everyone is nervously polite and not much gets done, through the painful but necessary 'storming' stage where arguments abound but the resultant friction helps to start things moving, on to the stage called 'norming' where team rules start to be established, and on (it is hoped) to the 'performing' stage.

It is convenient in team discussions to talk about 'where you are' (often a difficult topic) by relating it to a time on the clock. You can then move on to a discussion of what limitations that position involves, and then, where would you like to be within three, or six months – at what time of the clock?

Once you have an objective the drawing up of an action plan becomes a good deal easier – what Belbin roles will need to be in evidence to achieve our goal, what functional contributions (the G.R.O.W.s) will be required, and what team rules will we need to instigate? Team rules should be clear and simple –

193

such things as e-mail policy (must all e-mails be answered, do we approve of mailing groups?), meeting rules (timings, disciplines, are absences permitted?), and what to do with reports and minutes.

THE TEAM LEADER

It is unlikely that the team leader will be the boss. Most likely they will be a Key Account Manager with a team of individuals that do not work for them, might be senior to them, and are certainly more capable than them in their functional roles. Quite a challenge, but the leader still has to lead.

This is about having authority. Wielding authority as a result of a job title and hierarchical ranking – what we might call 'given' authority – is a relatively easy task, but even if we have a leader with such given authority in our supplier team there are better ways to go about things. The best authority is that which is earned and demonstrated through behaviours and attitudes, and that takes skill and a good deal of discipline.

There are many ways for a leader to earn and demonstrate authority; the following lists some of the more important in a cross-functional team environment:

- Demonstrate knowledge, but be honest about what isn't known; 'bluffing' is the fastest way to be found out...
- Consult the experts, and demonstrate an ability to listen.
- Involve senior management, but don't parade them as your 'licence to kill', nor let them steal your clothes...
- Demonstrate confidence, but always be realistic; 'boosting' is another sure way to be found out...
- Demonstrate 'Inclusive Leadership'; show interest in, and empathy for, the views of others; actively seek diverse opinions; explain decisions.
- Coach, don't tell.
- Demonstrate structure in your thinking and organization in your planning; having a well-prepared (and written) customer / investment / project plan is very important in this respect.
- Give regular feedback, communicate progress, don't hide from bad news and setbacks.
- Agree with the team the kind of leadership required.

This final point is an interesting one – asking the team how they want to be led – and the answers are often surprising.

Figure 11.12 shows the 'leadership spectrum', a choice of approaches ranging from 100 per cent directive through to the master of empowerment.

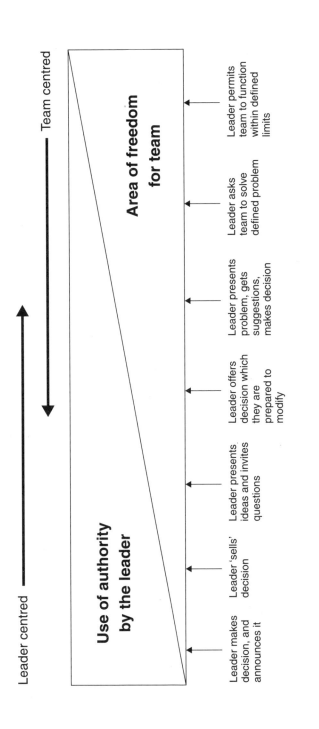

Figure 11.12 *The leadership spectrum*

The team leader could do worse than put this in front of the team at an early stage and ask for views. If the team is new, and the challenge is new, members might be inclined to vote for a leadership position towards the left, while making clear that they would like to see movement to the right as quickly as circumstances and experience allow. This is helpful, hugely so, to both leader and team, and like the Belbin tool provides us with a language to discuss things that are often difficult and so get put to one side. I call that the 'fester factor' and a good team leader should never leave things to fester.

Good leaders

Are good leaders born, or can they be made? I don't propose to express a view for fear of starting a whole new book at this point. Leadership is a big topic, generating more advice from business writers than perhaps any other subject in their field. There are books to help us find the lessons of leadership contained in the works of William Shakespeare, in the Holy Bible, even in the example of Sven-Goran Eriksson – I can only leave you to judge which of those might be more helpful.

In Chapter 12 we will look at one large 'slice' of the leadership task – the ability to lead change – to make new things happen. In the space available in this Chapter I will attempt no more than to suggest a top 10 list of thoughts that might help a leader prosper in the circumstances of a collaborative cross-functional team within the value machine:

- A good leader starts with a high level of self-awareness. They know what makes them tick, what turns them on and off, their strengths and their weaknesses (allowable or otherwise), how they like to make decisions, and how they like to work with others. This allows them to know what behaviours to curb and those to accentuate.
- A good leader is also aware of how they have become the way they are; what experiences have formed their beliefs and values. Such awareness goes a long way to help them understand the beliefs and values of others, and why that makes them who they are.
- A good leader aims to be inclusive, regarding a diversity of beliefs and values in a team as a good thing – something to be harnessed – not a handicap to be suppressed. Being inclusive means listening, taking note of opinions and seeking to build consensus. It doesn't mean agreeing with them all and ending up with a massive fudge.
- A good leader makes it clear why some opinions and ideas cannot be included in the team consensus, if such exclusion proves to be necessary.

- A good leader provides a clear vision of where they wish the team to be – 'what do we want and why do we want it?' – and involves the team in mapping out the path towards that vision – 'how will we get it?'
- A good leader understands the principles and requirements of change (see Chapter 12).
- A good leader knows when to empower and when to control – in both instances making appropriate use of performance management tools (see Chapter 12).
- A good leader ensures shared accountability for the activities and performance of the team, and equally, ensures shared recognition for success.
- A good leader coaches (see Chapter 12).
- A good leader is a communicator – which means listening twice as much as talking.

CUSTOMER COLLABORATION

Putting the team in front of the customer raises the stakes, heightens the challenge, and eases the progress. If that sounds a little contradictory, then an explanation is due. The stakes are raised as failure now involves the letting down of a customer. The challenge is heightened as the team enters a rather different business and working culture. Yet the progress is eased as the team make contact with reality – internal discussions about value propositions can seem quite vague and ethereal, but the discipline of a demanding customer either puts substance into them, or brings them crashing down. Teams usually work better in the face of *real* challenges.

Don't expect all team members to relish the prospect of customer contact. Many of them joined the company to be 'back-room' and this exposure can be daunting, stressful and unwelcome – and that goes for senior managers every bit as much as junior staff.

The sales professionals in the team have a double responsibility, one positive and one negative: to coach their colleagues, and not to bamboozle them with 'tales and anecdotes'. Sales people love to tell tales of vicious buyers, of the time they were thrown out on to the street – such things are not helpful. Use the tools described throughout this book when discussing the customer, and within the context they provide you can 'gossip' as much as you like – we might call this 'managed gossip' or 'gossip with a purpose...'.

Time should be given to training or coaching or briefing those involved with the customer, focusing on four key areas:

1. interpersonal skills;
2. commercial awareness;
3. legal and contractual acuity;
4. project management.

These are all big issues and might require professional help with either training or advice. It is not the intention of the following four sections to act as training manuals but simply to indicate why these skills and capabilities matter, and to suggest how progress might be made with their development.

INTERPERSONAL SKILLS

To make sure we get along...

It has often been said: it's easier to develop the interpersonal skills of an analytical chemist than it is to turn the best sales person into an analytical chemist. Apart from the implications that analytical chemists automatically lack interpersonal skills and that sales people automatically have them, I'm inclined to agree.

The mistake is to tell the analytical chemist (or accountant, or technical service manager or head of IT) that they are being sent on a course to turn them into sales people. That this might turn more people off than on should not be surprising – it suggests that their role and contribution is somehow secondary to that of the sales professionals.

Better perhaps to agree across the team that the world of the customer is a different world, requiring an observation of some rules and techniques – there is a particular etiquette to be observed. They are simple enough rules and techniques based on the simple truth that everyone, sales people included, will do a better job in front of the customer if they can develop a high level of 1:1 rapport, if they can build a relationship that allows them to learn, and if they can be persuasive. All three things are really bound up in one single all-important interpersonal skill – the ability to listen.

I knew a salesman once who gargled four times a day; he took a vacuum flask of hot salt water out on the road just for the purpose. It stopped him losing his voice, he told me.

'Vital tool of the trade,' he said, which had me worried; I'd heard he was a problem rep. I asked him why he took such care of his voice.

'Well,' he said, 'I average six calls a day, each one an average 45 minutes, that's four and a half hours.' He stopped, as if it was obvious, and I had to employ my special raised eyebrow technique. 'Well, four and a half hours, I mean, that's an awful lot of talking, isn't it?'

I had to agree, which is why he never did prosper in sales. He never quite got the hang of not talking – he was a natural to take the job of the speaking clock.

How do you rate as a listener, or rather, how do others rate you as a listener? Rank in order; your spouse, your children, the people who work for you, your boss, your best friend. Same order, and getting better as we go? If so then you are like many people, a good listener with the right motivation. To be a good listener all the time, especially with customers, is simple: always have the right motivation.

How do you aim to build rapport with the customer? By paying attention to them – by listening. How do you plan to learn from them? Again, quite simple, by listening. And to persuade them? Yes, listening again – having asked the right questions in the first place. Talking rarely persuades anyone; in fact with customers it can be quite the reverse, with a clever buyer sucking the talkative supplier into ever-greater indiscretions. Let's return to my 'gargling' salesman, and imagine how a 'conversation' with a buyer might proceed:

'Mr Prothero, I won't beat about the bush this morning because I've got some bad news, well, not so much bad as unpleasant… well, it's a price increase I'm afraid… yes, I know what you're thinking, that's another in quick succession on the last, but there are good reasons… raw materials have shot up of late, and I'm sure our competitors will be doing just the same… or going bust… Anyway, it applies from next month, so at least you've the chance to get an order in first… I do know what you're thinking, it's not the best time of year for a big order… Tell you what, I could slip one through for delivery next month, at the old price of course… or, I could stretch it a week or two beyond that… Look, I know you don't like this increase, nor do I. I was just saying to the other reps, only last week, stupid bloody idea, I said, but that's managers for you, never listen to a word we say… They'd listen to you mind. Perhaps I could try telling them your problem with this, and maybe they'll hold it off, in your case, after all you're a very important customer, one of our Key Accounts in fact… I could tell them we might even get a bigger order if we could shave a few percentage points off the current price… before the rise… whenever…'

At this point the buyer *awakens* from their silence:

'I've always said it, we poor buyers are no match for you silver-tongued sales folk…'

The best place to learn about interpersonal skills is from experience, and ideally matched with a good coach. A well-run training course, particularly if it includes all members of the supplier team and works on live circumstances and examples, can be a great way to develop shared skills and a common approach. Books on the other hand are of the least use – and yet the shelves are full of 'how to' guides on every aspect of the topic from negotiation skills through to neuro-linguistic-programming (NLP). Most of them are very worthy, some are excellent, but few people actually learn from reading them – we are talking here of skills to be learned through experience, observation and feedback.

So, rather than attempting to describe the many techniques that might be used, whether it be 'matching and mirroring' or 'high-gain questioning', I will close this section with a simple plea. Make sure that your business recognizes the importance of top-class interpersonal skills as a key ingredient in developing collaborative working relationships. And make sure that sufficient attention is given to developing the skills needed by your teams, and in the circumstances that they will be required.

COMMERCIAL AWARENESS

To make sure we make 'healthy' progress...

Don't send innocents into the lion's den. However much the talk may be about partnership don't ever forget that the customer is looking for the best outcome and 'loyalty' can be an expensive obstacle in that pursuit. Remember the tale of the pig and the chicken at the close of Chapter 6.

With those warnings ringing in our ears we should give some consideration to the commercial awareness of our teams. Are they OK with the customer, or do you fear sending them out without a chaperone? If it's the latter, don't send them – if they get suckered then you can only have yourself to blame.

It will be clear by now what I mean by 'commercial awareness'. I don't mean that they can read balance sheets (though that can be useful) or that they can do discounted cash flows on the backs of envelopes (another useful skill, mind), I mean: are they *streetwise*?

Collaboration can be a risky pursuit. You develop a solution with a customer, having done all the right things by understanding their true needs and matching them with your own capabilities, only to find that they have invited another supplier to take the solution to market, on grounds of price. It happens, and all too often.

The fault is not in the pursuit of collaboration but in the innocence with which it is sometimes pursued. Some customers just cannot be trusted – so don't attempt to build collaborative relationships with those customers. I'm reminded of the Tommy Cooper joke: 'Patient: Doctor, I've broken my arm in two different places. Doctor: Well don't go to those places.'

If you really feel that you cannot trust a customer then you will need to downgrade your ambitions of what can be achieved through a matched relationship – but first, aim to understand why they are so untrustworthy. Are they in difficulties that put them under unusual pressure? Can you do anything about that? Are you speaking with the wrong people? Can you do anything about that? Do they have a low opinion of your value as a supplier – what is there to be loyal for? Can you do anything about that? If you can act on these kinds of issue then the customer's trustworthiness might just improve.

Of course, even the most trustworthy of customers can sometimes stoop to dubious practices, and it may be that any supplier seriously intent on collaboration has to suffer the occasional knock alongside the benefits. We seek a healthy collaboration for sure, but that doesn't make the occasional head cold a reason for throwing it all in.

A vital demonstration of commercial awareness is to have the eye always on the goal, which is not, as some suppose, the delivery of the project to the customer, but the *delivery of the reward to the supplier*. It's like the old sales managers used to say: the sale isn't complete until the money is in the bank. The collaborative task is not completed until the supplier is rewarded for their brilliance.

Sometimes it is necessary to remind the customer of what you have done for them – they have short memories. Find reasons to remind them – reports, reviews, getting the recipients of the value to talk with others in their own business who might benefit in the same way, formal demonstrations, celebrations of success – this is all part of the continuing collaborative task, and all part of demonstrating a true commercial awareness.

I once spent the best part of a month devoting myself to one customer, helping them to develop new ways of displaying my products in a retail environment. I brought in plenty of colleagues to help with the task and I have to say we did a pretty good job. The customer was easy to work with and we enjoyed a high level of genuine collaboration.

Just three months later I was surprised to hear the customer say that they were feeling unloved: we never did anything special for them, they said. Resisting the temptation to remind them just how hard I had worked on their behalf I went away to think (in truth I think I went away to sulk, which can sometimes be the same thing). It just so happened that I had another customer, sufficiently distant not to be a competitor, who was keen on doing something similar, and so I arranged a visit to my first customer's store.

Sometimes magic really does happen. The new customer was impressed and called in my services (which incidentally now only required a week's work thanks to my team's enhanced experience) but even more importantly my first customer was delighted. They glowed with pride as they showed our guests around and I couldn't have come up with a better way of reminding them of what we had done together had I tried. Needless to say there were plenty more 'visits' after that, they became an important element of the 'post-project package'.

Can you train people to be commercially aware – to be streetwise? It would make a fascinating course, and the answer is, 'in parts'. The secret is to take care over managing peoples' expectations – supplier's and customer's. Ensure that the ambitions and objectives are realistic without damping down the essential flames of enthusiasm. Apply, in the language of Belbin (see above), the eye of the monitor evaluator. This is not to say 'be suspicious', just careful. Which brings us to the next topic…

LEGAL AND CONTRACTUAL ACUITY

To make sure we don't fall into any bear traps…

In matters of customer contracts, particularly those involving joint development projects, seek professional advice early. Yes, lawyers hold things up and can bog you down. Yes, it is true that if you ever have to bring out the contract to argue a point then the relationship has probably already failed. Yes, we all hate the jargon. So why bother with the legal stuff in the first place?

The great thing about getting contracts drawn up is the way that this disciplines the mind from the start. Lawyers ask the damnedest questions about things we had never considered; sometimes they take us down irrelevant alleys, other times they are spot on. Once it's all done, put it away in a drawer and get on with the business of 'making it happen' happy in the knowledge that you have planned for all eventualities.

This is of course a job for the experts. Don't expect individual members of the team to become lawyers overnight (I'm not sure who is the more dangerous, the amateur lawyer or the amateur accountant), and don't let anyone push you into bypassing the proper channels in order to get things speeded up. It is a common customer 'device' to urge such an approach, in order to meet some vital deadline. Part of being 'commercially aware' is being able to spot the difference between true customer impatience and manufactured customer guile.

PROJECT MANAGEMENT

To make sure it all happens…

Doubtless your own business already has a number of project management tools in use. Ask the marketing people if there is a new product development (NPD) process in place. Ask the operations folk, or the R&D team; they are often the experts.

The same probably applies in the customer's operations, so we have no shortage of tools or processes from which to choose.

Then, almost before you know it, a battle royal breaks out over who has the best tool, the most appropriate tool, the most effective tool, the easiest to use tool; its us or them…

This one is easy, at least to begin with. The politically astute supplier will surely recognize the customer's methodologies to be the best, regardless of the technical arguments for and against, simply because they are the customer's. Choosing their methodology is the most likely way to gain access and speed progress, but look out for the problems in your own organization – there will be plenty of complaints about poor processes, those 'amateurs', and how we wouldn't do it like that round here…

If this happens, try to remain calm and remind people what this is all meant to be about. If people will only trim a little from their own idea of perfection it is surprising what good can be seen in other approaches, and what progress can be made through compromise and adaptation.

There are perhaps some essentials that we should ensure are in place in whatever system is used, and most approaches will include these, though they may use different terminologies.

There should be a clear agreement at the outset of the purpose of the project, making clear what are the allowable trade-offs between the time required, the costs involved and the quality sought. Clarity over this 'eternal triangle' as it is sometimes called will be of huge importance later down the track, as we will see.

There should be an assessment of risks: what could go wrong, what assumptions does success rely upon, and what are the contingency plans in the events of the almost inevitable change to circumstances? Again, clarity at this point will pay dividends at a later stage.

The project should be laid out as a clear list of tasks, with appropriate milestones of progress and a clear assessment of what are usually called the 'dependencies', that is: what has to have happened with previous tasks for this next task to be possible? This is the 'critical path' and is usually laid out with the help of a Gantt chart, an essential tool for communicating dependencies and monitoring progress.

Then come the progress reports and the inevitable problems: the hold-ups, the breaks in the chain of dependencies, the changes to circumstances and confounding of assumptions. Any project at such a moment can be threatened but those managed between two separate entities are at particular risk. Arguments can develop quickly, the fingers of blame are pointed and before you know it budgets and resources are removed; end of project.

This is when that early care over risk assessment, contingency planning and agreement over the trade-offs of the 'eternal triangle' will pay dividends. Do you have a contingency, what did you agree about increasing resources if necessary, and who was to provide them? What was our view on extending timetables versus reducing costs, or downgrading the quality of the outcome if that can save time and money?

Such planning for bad times is of especial importance in the kind of collaborative partnerships we are describing. Within your own organization problems can be overcome by appealing to a higher authority – in joint development projects there are two higher authorities involved, and that can lead to all sorts of problems. Best not to have to make the appeal in the first place…

MAKING GOOD OUR VALUE

If these short discussions on four different elements of the collaborative task have made collaboration sound a little less, well, collaborative than you might have imagined, then I make no apologies for a small injection of realism. The best business collaborations are always firmly based in the realms of the possible and the practical. So, rather than causing you to fear the process, I hope that some of the caution expressed leads you on instead to more effective outcomes.

The concept behind the value machine is essentially a selfish one. The value machine business is concerned with its own health, aiming to protect and improve it through displays of concern over the health of others. These displays can of course be entirely genuine in themselves (and for the most part it is hoped that they will be) but the selfish outcome remains – we're in it for us.

Our selfishness must extend beyond the birth of value – the point at which it is delivered to the customer – we must now ensure that our 'child' grows up as planned, to the benefit of *both* parents, customer and supplier.

The supplier must ensure that the customer uses its new value properly, and that they secure the benefits promised and expected. That may involve training customer staff, or the setting up of progress reviews and 'health checks'. The original value proposition may need tweaking and amending from time to time – the 'new improved' approach – and the customer will certainly need reminding of what you have done for them. That way the supplier ensures and protects their reward from the customer over the longer term.

The supplier must also ensure that the new value is used well within their own organization – enhancing internal efficiencies and building new and more effective capabilities. What we achieve with one customer today we should be aiming to achieve with others tomorrow.

> This is hardly a new idea of course. Back in the early years of the 20th century WH Lever was keen to explain how his experiences with selling Sunlight soap in the USA were hugely important to the development of its sales in the UK (the original market). The USA taught him how to add new value into a mundane product and having discovered and created a revolution in sales and marketing technique he sought to clone his creation far and wide. The rest we know.

A REAL-WORLD PROBLEM...
OR JUST GOOD NEGOTIATION?

Suppose, through customer collaboration, you have developed a great new product or idea. What then if our targeted and matched customer demands exclusivity? They might very well be expected to if they are investing some of their own efforts into a joint development of a new solution. Even if they don't demand exclusivity, how will they feel if the idea they developed in partnership with you turns up in their competitors some time later?

I have repeatedly said that a supplier should aim to capitalize on their new capabilities with a broader group of customers, but if exclusivity is a must, then that is one benefit of the value machine to be forgone. Having said that however, if exclusivity is a must, then there are still two responses to be made – for how long, and what do we get in return? Might you agree your own version of exclusivity – a sole supplier arrangement, and for the same period of time?

While exclusivity deals might stop you repeating the exact same proposition elsewhere, they cannot stop you from becoming cleverer. Some customers may even be smart enough to see that through a process of joint development they will improve your capabilities, and might even ask for a better deal based on that benefit. You may choose to give them that better deal, but if you do, surely that must impact in some way on their demands for exclusivity?

The real world of the negotiation remains, even in the most collaborative of relationships. In fact, the most collaborative relationships will more than likely result from the fact that a rational and cooperative basis of negotiation has been agreed in advance. An excellent book, *Getting to Yes*, by Roger Fisher and William Ury, lays out such an approach based on four key principles:

1. people – attend to the people issues first;
2. interests – focus on interests, not positions;
3. options – generate a variety of possibilities before deciding what to do;
4. criteria – insist that the result be based on some objective standard.

For me, the key is in the second principle – not allowing negotiations to become arm-wrestling contests over separate lists of demands, but seeking to find what common interests lie behind those lists. If ever there was fertile ground for such common interests then surely it is in the world of collaborative partnerships in pursuit of mutual benefit through enhanced value propositions, in the context of the value machine?

12

Leading the change

In Chapter 2 we spoke of the pivotal role, quite literally as shown in Figure 12.1, of the leadership team in creating and sustaining the value machine.

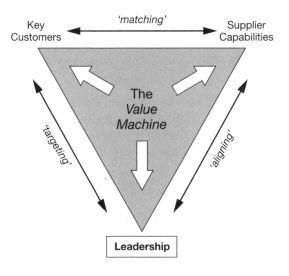

Figure 12.1 *The pivotal role of leadership*

One of the key tasks of the leadership team is to maintain the right balance, which, as we noted, doesn't always mean equilibrium. There are times when the leadership team should be actively encouraging the business to lean more towards their customers, and times when it must shift the balance in the other direction – the circumstance and situation is all. It may even be that if the right balance has been achieved, and the environment is stable, then a 'steady as she goes' message is required from the leadership team. At this point they become a normal *management team*, illustrated in Figure 12.2 by flattening out the point at the bottom of the triangle in pursuit of that stability.

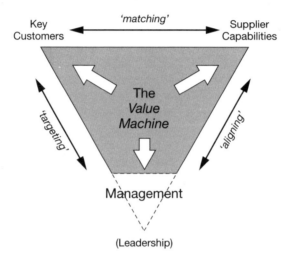

Figure 12.2 *'Steady as she goes' management*

This makes an important distinction between *managing* and *leading*. Managers are managers through their position in the hierarchy and remain so whatever the circumstances and whatever their quality and whatever their staff might feel about them. Leaders, on the other hand, are only leaders if they are recognized as such, and accepted as such. The day-to-day operations of a business can get by with managers, but if there is need for change then quality leadership becomes essential.

In the context of the value machine, leadership is required to remove obstacles, to effect the correct balance at any time, and to harness the right behaviours for the triple tasks of focusing, aligning and matching to take place. Change is a constant in all of those activities.

LEADING CHANGE

People normally talk about 'change management' – having made my distinction between managing and leading you will understand why I prefer to speak of 'leading change'. Change isn't part of the day-to-day management processes, it is something that more than likely tears people away from those things, threatening to cause instability or chaos, and almost certainly generating stress. So there are going to have to be some pretty good reasons why people *should* change, and some pretty effective leadership to persuade them of those reasons and to guide them through the process *without* instability and chaos, and with the minimum of stress (some stress is necessary for the purpose, and in some cases even a little instability can help, but chaos? Hardly ever.).

There is a good and proven process to follow, to be discussed below, but first a brief comment on the reasons why people and organizations do change. In essence it is explained by the *change equation*, illustrated in Figure 12.3.

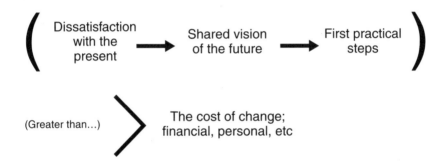

Figure 12.3 *The change equation*

Change happens when this whole string of factors is in place. Miss any one of them and the obstacles to change will more than likely win the day.

People need to be dissatisfied with what they have already in order even to think about changing. Sometimes they have to be very dissatisfied. It is the task of the leadership team to identify what dissatisfaction exists, and if it isn't sufficient to the purpose, to add to it. It is rather as professional advertisers do in making us want to change to buy their product – making us feel too fat, too old, too tired, too unattractive.

Of course, if that were all that the admen and the bosses did then they would be very unpopular people. For change to happen they must go on to the second step in the equation, providing a shared vision of the future. Wouldn't it be great if you were slimmer, felt younger, were more active, were

209

more attractive? Wouldn't it be great if we weren't losing customers, weren't getting caned by the competition, and didn't always feel under pressure to cut prices? The shared vision aims to show how things could be, and the key word here is 'shared'. You know what you want them to think, but do they?

> When Alexander Graham Bell invented the telephone he toured the USA showing it off to what he hoped would be interested businessmen. After one such session, he was approached by an apparent enthusiast: 'Mr Bell, I really like your new toy. It's my daughter's birthday party tomorrow and I would be very grateful if you would come along to show it.'
>
> Well, the great man was incensed: 'It is not a toy!' he exploded. 'Don't you realize that this will revolutionize communications and your business? Just think, with one of these you can talk to a customer 300 miles away.'
>
> The businessman thought for a moment and then answered: 'But, Mr Bell, I don't have any customers 300 miles away...'

If people don't know what is possible then it is unreasonable to expect them to share your vision without a good deal of help. Communicating the vision is a vital task.

Even now, people might still resist change, they still might not buy your product or accept your business rescue package, perhaps because they don't think it's practical or even possible. It's a great vision, but it's all too much. It is necessary to show that it *is* practical and that it *is* possible; you *can* lose weight, we *can* win back those customers, but not all at once – one step at a time. This is what we mean by the 'first practical steps'.

One last hurdle; all of this dissatisfaction, shared vision, and first practical steps must add up to something greater than the cost of change. The cost might be money, or it might be ego, or a dozen other things. Now the mathematicians among you will have spotted that this isn't in fact an *equation* at all, but an *inequality* – one side has to be greater than the other for it to work – and that suggests the options open to those seeking to lead change. First option: reduce the cost of change. Great if you can, but you may just be stuck with it. Second option: increase the levels of dissatisfaction, make the vision yet more enticing and more genuinely shared, make the first steps even easier to take... If this second option is your task then it will be even more important to have a good process and a great leadership team.

THE CHANGE PROCESS

I will suggest an eight-step process, shown in Figure 12.4. This is a process based on the work of John Kotter and used successfully by my own company with many clients over many years:

1. Establish clear reasons for change
2. Get the right people on board to lead and facilitate the change process
3. Create the vision
4. Communicate the vision
5. Empowerment
6. Have a plan for success and a plan for failure
7. Consolidate improvements and produce more change
8. Institutionalize the new approaches

Figure 12.4 *The change process*

Feel free to modify the language (as we have done from John Kotter's original), to expand on some of the steps, perhaps even to add some extra ones, but take care before removing any – this comes as a full working package.

1. Establish clear reasons for change

Be crystal clear about why change is necessary, injecting that clarity with a sense of urgency. I have some clients who ask: what is the burning platform? – meaning: what is fast disappearing from beneath our feet if we don't do something about things? We are talking of course of promoting dissatisfaction with the status quo, as required in the change equation (see Figure 12.2).

There are so many reasons why you and your team might be dissatisfied that I mention only a very few, and almost at random:

- we're losing customers…
- just lost our most important account…
- sales are plummeting…
- profits are plummeting…
- our competitors are gaining ground on us…
- we're failing to seize new opportunities…

- there is growing customer dissatisfaction…
- we have an unresponsive organization…
- we constantly squabble internally over priorities and budgets and accountabilities…
- we're not focused…
- we're not aligned…
- we're doing new things but not getting new rewards…
- our pace of new product development is slowing…
- our operational efficiencies are dropping…

2. Get the right people on board to lead and facilitate the change process

Don't work alone – nobody is that good – gather a broad team. They will act variously as guides, champions, consultants, enablers and implementers. Getting the leadership team on board goes without saying. There will doubtless be some key managers to involve, perhaps from those functions most impacted by the change or needing to effect the most change themselves. They represent key influencers and in any change programme or persuasion task (and at this point of the process they are one and the same thing) it is always wise to have the key influencers on board. This doesn't just mean the people who agree with you, of course. Aim to involve those with good reason to oppose the change – the laggards, the blockers and the luddites. They may not make easy bedfellows, but better to have them inside the team than outside throwing stones. It may sound rather Machiavellian (and indeed it is straight from his precepts), but if you have opponents, bring them into the fold where you can keep an eye on them, control their behaviours, and maybe even convert them. You may have noticed that Prime Ministers and Presidents often appoint their number one 'challenger' as their deputy – now I wonder why they should do such a thing…

Don't make important decisions in ivory towers (or boardrooms) but aim to involve and build as broad a coalition as possible. People are much better persuaded through involvement than by instruction. The price you pay may be that things get slowed down a little, that different words are used, and that some different actions may get taken. The good news is that people will be supporting not resisting, which leads to better news – this will actually speed things up in the end – and perhaps on to even better news – this broader involvement may just lead to better, more practical, more relevant and more workable ideas.

3. Create the vision

This whole book has been about the vision of the value machine, so you should have plenty of material to create your own version! Of course, your own vision should be a good deal shorter – half a dozen good clear sentences should suffice. The vision is about distilling the essence of three big questions: what do we want, why do we want it, and how will we get it?

Imbue your answers with a sense of urgency, express them in language that suggests practicality and possibility, and you will have a workable vision serving three purposes. First, and most obviously, it allows others to understand why change is needed. Second, it allows individuals to identify their own role in making it happen. Third, and perhaps most importantly to the success of the project, it gives the leadership team the confidence to 'let go'. There is always a danger that those who know what they want grow impatient with those that don't understand (those who 'don't get it') and start to take over – the very 'command and control' behaviours that we aim to avoid at step 5 of this process. A clear vision gives everyone the confidence to get on with things with the minimum of imposed control and the maximum of empowered creativity.

4. Communicate the vision

It is easier to communicate six good clear sentences than a whole book full of stuff, hence the need for brevity. But there is more to this than keeping things short – this is perhaps the most important step of all eight – this is where you aim to inspire people to become involved, and to motivate them to get on with it in the face of all the obstacles. This is where alignment truly starts.

Some tips. Don't be dull, but don't be facile – people like to see a spark of something in their leaders but they don't want them to be silly, and most of all they don't want them to be patronizing. Make sure you exemplify the attitudes and behaviours expected of the people involved in making change happen. Ask for people's own feelings on what's wrong and what could be right before lecturing them on yours (and don't lecture them in any case) – you may just be surprised to hear that they were closer to your thoughts than you imagined. When you do express your own views, ask people what they think, and don't look at them as if their days are numbered if at first they don't appear to agree.

Using new language

If you want new things thought and done, consider using new language to describe them. Words matter.

In Chapter 1 we observed that the value machine would require a new language to express its motivations and mechanics.

In Chapter 2 we saw how old and inappropriate language created dangerous barriers to thinking. In the case of the suppliers that spoke dismissively of their retail customers' 'own labels, private labels, and no labels' it was the way in which they spoke of their customers that created a mental block to any form of collaboration. 'Our biggest customers are also our largest competitors,' they said. Deadly words.

In Chapter 3 we discussed how the language of individual functions contributed to the creation of 'silos' within the business. A common language within a function is an important part of how it bonds, but it also leaves other functions looking and *sounding* alien.

In Chapter 6 we saw how a simple word, 'support', when applied to functions (as in 'support functions') might create a sense of hierarchy and subservience never intended. Similarly, in Chapter 10 the phrase 'internal customer' was seen to be too easily an excuse not to think about *real* customers. It is a phrase (or weasel words I would rather call it) used by those functions sometimes described as being 'non-customer-facing' – a more ugly term in the context of the value machine I cannot imagine.

In Chapter 8 it was suggested that adopting the customer's language would do much to facilitate the matching process across Diamond Teams. It would certainly have helped our beer supplier in Chapter 9 earnestly trying to impress on their customer the good news of them buying more 'barrels' than the previous year…

Whatever words you use, keep them simple. Jargon is a killer and too easily the brunt of cynical mockery. Words like 'target', 'match', and 'align' are I hope good words – they were certainly approved of by one of my clients who said that they were good simple English, 'like what I speak'…

Aim to be pictorial, even symbolic. Much can be made of the vocabulary and imagery of the value machine – the analogy with a steam engine introduced in Chapter 7 has plenty of potential in this respect, not least the idea of breathing life into its workings through the fire of people.

If you want to turn your organization 'upside down', why not start, like the new boss in Chapter 10, literally by turning the organization chart upside down?

Aim to express your intentions by the language you use. If you want to work 'with' customers, consider the alternatives to the 'doing to' 4 P's suggested in Chapter 8.

Finally, does the value machine work through *internal* and *external* functions? This is getting worryingly close to *customer-facing* and *non-customer-facing*, and I dread to think which way the latter are looking…

5. Empowerment

There is probably more tosh spoken about empowerment than any other topic in the business community, and mostly by those who have no intention of letting go the strings of command and control (or, as often, have no *ability* to do so). Empowerment happens when the bosses are confident in their plan, are confident in their team, and are confident in the outcomes – otherwise expect high levels of command and control. This actually makes good sense, as the alternative is chaos and poor performance.

So a good place to start is with building that confidence, which will come from each step covered so far – the inclusion of diverse opinions, the clarity of purpose, and the sense of alignment behind the vision. More must follow, and will do throughout this change process as we move into areas such as planning for quick wins, building on success, and enjoying the fruits of that success. In a sense the whole change process is designed to build confidence step by step, and in both directions; the organization's in their leadership, and the leadership's in their organization.

For people to be empowered to act on the vision all sorts of obstacles must be removed. It is not enough to say: you are now empowered to remove those obstacles – if that were truly possible then they would have been dealt with long ago. Revisit the sins and obstacles discussed in Chapter 10 and ask yourself, honestly: how many of these need action from the top?

Performance management

Remove those processes and systems that undermine the vision. If you want cross-functional supplier teams to act with greater collaborative and entrepreneurial spirit then be rid of those performance measures for monitoring and controlling and improving 'inputs', and put in place measures to promote creativity and flexibility and improved 'outcomes'. A struggling sales team might be monitored and controlled by 'input measures' such as the number of calls per day, or the number of miles driven per call, and all too often because their bosses don't trust them to get on with things on their own initiative. A sales team in a true value machine should rebel if such measures are still in place. Aim to measure the outputs of their activities – the decision-making units penetrated, the opportunities uncovered, the collaborative projects initiated and the business improvements achieved. Harder to measure, but then if you were looking for things easy to measure you would set up a monitor of tyre pressure before and after the call...

Empowerment isn't about abandonment. Performance management tools are fine – they simply have to be appropriate to the task. People will need guidance, some might even want direction and instruction – look again at the leadership spectrum at Figure 11.12 in Chapter 11 and think about what nature of leadership is required. In the true spirit of empowerment, ask those about to be led just how they might like to be led.

Coaching

Empowerment isn't about putting new ideas and capabilities into peoples' heads; it's about getting out what ideas and capabilities are already in there but too often are smothered by the blankets of command and control. (Replace the word 'empowerment' with 'leadership' and the sentence stands unaltered.) One of the single most important things to be sure of at this point – a critical success factor if there ever was one – is that the skills and habits of *coaching* are alive and well throughout the organization.

Coaching is not the same as instructing, or training. Instructing and training start from the following premise: I, the instructor or trainer, know more about this than you do, so shut up and listen because it will be good for you (or something like that). Coaching starts from an absolutely opposite premise: you, the person I am coaching, are very likely to be more capable than me and better at this than me, and my job is to get that capability out of you. If Tiger Wood's coach played golf better than Tiger Wood's, he'd be doing it.

Of all the leadership and management skills that might be developed in order to make the value machine buzz with life, I would vote for coaching skills to be in number one position.

6. Have a plan for success and a plan for failure

Both will happen, so you may as well be prepared. Plan deliberately to create some quick wins, some customer successes, some project successes, some internal successes, and then celebrate them like crazy. Nothing builds confidence more speedily than seeing things go well – so make sure that when they do go well, people get to know about them.

In celebrating the successes make sure that reward is given where it is due. That almost certainly means rewarding teams more often than individuals (though the latter isn't banned by any means), and this doesn't have to mean money or promotion; in fact, simple recognition will almost certainly work better in keeping the wheels of change moving. Prepare a PR campaign that reports on progress and gives a suitable vehicle for such recognition. And in the spirit of the value machine's collaborative partnerships, think about how you might be able to involve the customer as a part of the PR campaign.

Aim to recognize and reward the kind of behaviours you seek every much as bit as you recognize and reward actual successes – and preferably both in tandem.

Learning from failure

In defeat: defiance, to quote Sir Winston Churchill. Aim to learn from the setbacks – failures usually have more and better lessons than successes. Consult with those involved, not in the spirit of a witch-hunt but in the spirit of improvement. Good coaching skills will once more be invaluable at such times.

In Chapter 2 we introduced the idea of the successful leader as something of a _political entrepreneur_; someone with a good nose for an opportunity and an equally good nose for what is possible. 'Leadership is the art of the possible' – cliché of all clichés perhaps, but true for all that. Any programme of change should have within it a good degree of slack to cope with the setbacks, and a planned intention to use those setbacks as new spurs to progress. Sir Winston Churchill (again) was a little more cynical perhaps when saying that: 'success is about going from failure to failure without any loss of enthusiasm'.

7. Consolidate improvements and produce more change

Building on step 6, celebrate success at every opportunity, and then use it to guide the creation of new approaches and processes. Learn from the failures in much the same way, modifying approaches and processes as you proceed.

As things get better use the evidence of those improvements to add speed to the process, like the snowball gathering momentum on its way downhill. This is now more than a PR exercise, this is about tangible and quantifiable enhancements to efficiency and effectiveness, to be shared across the business in practical applications.

This is the time to start forcing the pace, but recognize that this is still new for some people – don't assume immediate acceptance of new ways on account of an isolated success. If they're not listening after the third example of success then you have problems – revisit steps 1 through 6.

8. Institutionalize the new approaches

As new behaviours bring new successes aim to institutionalize them, to make them the new status quo. Once the leadership team are confident that this is so, they can safely leave the management of the business in the hands of the managers, effectively flattening the bottom point of the value machine triangle as we saw in Figure 12.2. But the leadership role remains, as indicated in that Figure, to watch for change in the environment that might call on another tipping of the triangle in one direction or the other, and another programme of change.

It becomes clear at this point why any change process must first harness the acceptance and support of the managers, which takes us back to step 2 in the process.

One of the larger UK pharmaceutical companies decided to take their entire sales team through a programme of training entitled 'New Account Management' aiming to help the sales professionals develop a new and deeper knowledge of their customer base, from which they would decide new priorities for customer contact plans and sales outcomes. It was all very much on the lines, as discussed in Chapter 6, of recognizing a spectrum of account types and so a spectrum of priorities and commitments. Most importantly it would free them from the shackles of the blanket call rate and coverage model that had bedevilled them for years.

The training went well and the sales people went back to their territories enthused and eager for change, only to find that their sales managers, who had not been on the course, were immediately chasing them for weekly call reports and questioning them on why call rates were changing, and why they hadn't been to Hospital X for so long, and why they were spending so much time with Hospital Y...

You can guess at the final outcome I'm sure.

Change is certainly about winning hearts and minds but it is necessary to win them in the right order. Any change, if we want it to stick, has to work through the management hierarchy from top down. Those glorious examples of change percolating up from the bottom in bubbles of inspired enthusiasm are as rare as cuckoo nests and about as easy to effect and lead as herding cats. They make for good reading, but little else.

There is of course a danger here that by establishing a new status quo we may be establishing a new obstacle (and a well-built one at that) to future change. You must decide: is change a constant for you – in which case the idea of institutionalizing anything is probably anathema – or are there moments when you can say that enough is enough, now let's get down to working with our new skills and to our new processes?

Afterword

And so it is done; the processes, skills and behaviours of a true value machine are embedded in your organization. Doubtless this will have been at the cost of some frayed nerves and a good few dented egos, but that's surely a price worth paying for the gains in operational efficiency and overall business effectiveness? If you could relate each percentage point of improved profitability to the particular egos in questions it would show a handsome return.

Of course, nothing *physical* has changed. The customer, the functions and the leadership team still occupy their separate spaces – we have not formed a commune – but we *have* bound them together by a concept, and by a state of mind.

This is the simple idea that by focusing the efforts of purposely collaborative cross-functional teams on to a small number of very carefully chosen customers, a whole host of benefits ensue.

It begins with an enhanced understanding of the customer, and of our own business capabilities in relation to that customer. It proceeds to the identification of new opportunities that can be translated into the creation of new value. The way in which we now view the rewards for that creativity is perhaps the most important part of the value machine concept. The customer gets their solution. We get the business, perhaps at a premium price, and perhaps with an increase in volume and share. Not bad, but we can do better, through gaining better access to people and future opportunities, and by building genuine customer loyalty. Not bad again, but there is better yet, and perhaps the real objective of the exercise: through the creation of new solutions and value we improve our own capabilities, so enhancing our value to *all* customers.

The most impressive evidence of all this, from the targeted customer's perspective, will probably be something beyond the value received from the supplier's products and services, and that is the value received from the relationship itself. It is the relationship that makes it all possible and sustains it over time. When the relationship is seen to have value *in itself,* we have the mark of a true value machine.

From the supplier's perspective the most impressive evidence of all this may be something to which most people will not give a second thought: the way that we talk about ourselves and our customers. To hear the language of collaboration used with customers, and across your whole business, will not only be hugely gratifying, but will be important proof that after all your efforts to become a value machine, you have at last arrived.

Getting further help

If reading this book has enthused you enough to want to turn your own business into a working value machine then don't plough a solo course. Speak with people who have trodden this path before. If you are right at the start of the journey aim to speak with colleagues who may share your thoughts – lend them this book to read for a start (the publisher wanted me to say 'buy one for them' but I live in the real world…).

I will be delighted if you wish to contact me, or any of my colleagues, for any further thoughts or advice, and our contact details are below. My company, INSIGHT Marketing and People Ltd, works globally with a broad range of clients on all of the issues covered by this book and we may be able to help you with consultancy or training, and if we are unable to match your specific interests then be sure that we will point you in the right direction. Our own focus is on the following areas, all within the context of the value machine:

- developing business strategy;
- Key and Global Account Management;
- strategic selling;
- leadership;
- coaching;
- managing diversity;
- team building;

- creative thinking;
- leading change;
- influencing skills;
- negotiation skills.

CONTACT DETAILS

e-mail: peter.cheverton@insight-mp.com
customer.service@insight-mp.com

Mailing address:
INSIGHT Marketing and People Ltd
INSIGHT House
11 Stour Close
Slough SL1 T2U
Royal Berkshire
United Kingdom
Telephone: +44 (0)1753 822990

FURTHER READING

Key Account Management, by Peter Cheverton, published by Kogan Page
Global Account Management, by Peter Cheverton, published by Kogan Page
Key Marketing Skills, by Peter Cheverton, published by Kogan Page
Understanding Brands, by Peter Cheverton, published by Kogan Page
Not Bosses but Leaders, by John Adair, published by Kogan Page
Team Roles at Work, by Meredith Belbin, published by Butterworth Heinemann
Marketing Plans, by Prof Malcolm MacDonald, published by Butterworth Heinemann
The Discipline of Market Leaders, by M Treacy and F Weirsema, published by HarperCollins
Getting to Yes, by Roger Fisher and William Ury, published by Random House

Index